Praise for *Reclaiming Rest*
by Kate H. Rademacher

"With great effectiveness Kate Rademacher shows us both *why* the practice of keeping Sabbath is so crucial and *how* it can become a reality. A much-needed read for anyone who takes seriously the way of Love to which Jesus calls us—which includes the call to rest."

—Rev. Michael Curry, presiding bishop of The Episcopal Church and author of *Love Is the Way: Holding on to Hope in Troubling Times*

"If you do not recognize yourself in the first few pages of this compelling, sage, and down-to-earth book, trust me: Rademacher is going to call your name before she is through. At the moment, I cannot think of another book that makes a better case for wedding faithful activism to equally faithful rest."

—Barbara Brown Taylor, author of *Always a Guest* and *An Altar in the World*

"What a refreshing invitation, as timely as a cool drink of water on an overheated day. In these exhausting, driven, and shattered times, may we heed her call to honor ourselves and God by humbly retreating to good Sabbath rest."

—Patricia Raybon, author of *I Told the Mountain to Move: Learning to Pray So Things Change* and *The One Year God's Great Blessings Devotional*

"Here, we have prose that snaps, practical suggestions coupled with deep wisdom, spirituality connected to politics, and, finally, not just an invitation to a single practice called Sabbath-keeping, but rather an invitation to a more faithful way of life."

—Lauren F. Winner, author of *The Dangers of Christian Practice* and *Wearing God*

"Kate Rademacher's writing is a delight, and she brings science, spirituality, and common sense together in just the way people like me most relate to and enjoy. This book could be what saves your sanity in these stressful times."

—Brian D. McLaren, author of *Faith after Doubt*

"In *Reclaiming Rest*, Kate H. Rademacher both inspires and challenges us to restore the deep freedom that we receive in keeping a Sabbath day. She is an eloquent writer and a natural storyteller, which makes this book as delightful to read as it is spiritually nourishing."

—Carl McColman, author of *Unteachable Lessons* and *Eternal Heart*

"In an era of exhaustion, Kate Rademacher has written the book we all need to read. By seamlessly weaving theology, history, and personal narrative, Rademacher creates a compelling case for the original intent of the Sabbath: not only to restore our week but to restore our lives."

—Kathy Izard, author of *The Hundred Story Home*
and founder of Women I Faith & Story

"The church so desperately needs the Sabbath. But so does the world. And creation. Rademacher has picked up something of the ways of Jesus here that the global church so desperately needs to hear."

—A.J. Swoboda, PhD, assistant professor of Bible, Theology,
and World Christianity at Bushnell University and
author of *Subversive Sabbath* and *After Doubt*

"In *Reclaiming Rest*, Rademacher not only shares important insights drawn from her own personal stories of struggle for Sabbath, but also offers practical situations, examples, and advice that others can learn from and follow."

—Brian Allain, founder of Writing for Your Life, Publishing
in Color, and Compassionate Christianity

"In candid and relatable prose, Rademacher describes her own journey to a Sabbath practice, while deftly exploring an array of rest-related themes, from theologies of social justice to strategies for abstaining from our screens."

—Erica C. Witsell, author of the
award-winning novel *Give*

"In sharing the roots and evolution of her Sabbath practice, Rademacher offers a compelling rationale and road map for restoration at a time when it is desperately needed. She extends a warm invitation to join her in a more faithful and authentic way of living— through the sacred, revolutionary act of rest."

—Elizabeth Futrell, coauthor of *Roar:
True Tales of Women Warriors*

"On almost every page, *Reclaiming Rest* made me reflect on who I am, what I do, why I do it, and where my work and life are taking me. Now as I intentionally work toward my own Sabbath practice, my new mantra is: 'Work. Reflect. Rest. Reflect. Repeat.'"

—Dr. Funmilola OlaOlorun, Women's Health
Researcher, College of Medicine, University
of Ibadan, Ibadan, Nigeria

Reclaiming Rest

Reclaiming Rest

*The Promise of Sabbath, Solitude,
and Stillness in a Restless World*

Kate H. Rademacher

Broadleaf Books
Minneapolis

To my brothers, Chris and Andrew,
with admiration, love, and gratitude

And to my Sabbath buddy, Carol

Contents

Introduction

FOR THE LAST TEN YEARS, I have been jotting down comments friends and colleagues make about how exhausted they feel in their everyday lives. I note them in my journal or on scraps of paper on my desk. The comments have been made by women and men, people who are single and married, people without children and people with one or more kids. As anecdotal data points, they reveal a troubling pattern:

> "I just don't think I can keep doing this for another twenty or thirty years."
> "I think working on that last grant proposal nearly broke me."
> "I have to get out of this job. Maybe if they offered a sabbatical or something, I could stay."
> "When I was unemployed and looking for work, I felt like I just didn't *deserve* to rest."
> "Living outside of the United States for a year made me realize I can't live like this anymore. I need more *tranquilidad* in my life."
> "Maybe our daughters' generation will figure out how to balance it all. We certainly haven't."

My colleague Maya made that last comment as we were standing in the hallway at work. She was leaning against the wall, resting the side of her head against it. Maya and I work at a large international nonprofit organization that focuses on global development and public health. As I faced Maya that day in the hall, we both complained that the pace of our lives felt unsustainable. It was incredibly difficult to juggle all of our responsibilities and even more difficult to do it all well. And she was fed up. Our generation had been trying for decades to figure out how to achieve "work-life balance," she said, but we had failed. In that moment, she was ready to acknowledge defeat and hand the problem over to the next generation to solve.

But I am not ready to give up. I don't want to leave this quagmire unresolved for our kids. My daughter, Lila, is fourteen years old. She is brilliant and kind and wise and sensitive and funny. And she is about to start ninth grade, which is the year that I first started having chronic panic attacks. My clinical anxiety lasted nearly a decade before I got it under control. Since that time, I have wondered about the same core set of questions: How do we achieve "balance"? What does that even mean? How can we get our individual and collective anxiety and exhaustion under control? How can we live *differently*?

While I've learned ways to curtail—or at least manage—my own anxiety, I remain worried for my daughter. I don't want her to have to go through the same painful process I did. This fear is what motivates me to keep searching for answers. I want to model for her how we can both work hard and rest deeply.

Like many of my peers, I have a lot I want to accomplish. I want to make the world a better place, and I want to make time to exercise. I want to keep in touch with my friends and family who live far away, and I want to be present to my husband, stepson, and daughter at home. I want to volunteer at church, and I want time for myself. I want to "do it all," but aiming for that goalpost often leaves me frazzled, depleted, and cranky.

After struggling for decades with how to balance it all, I stumbled upon a simple, ancient, and intuitive practice. In my early thirties, I was in the middle of an unexpected spiritual conversion experience that eventually led to my baptism and confirmation in the Episcopal Church. As part of that process, I adopted a weekly routine that ultimately became life transforming: I started observing the Sabbath.

In reading about the theology of Sabbath, I realized that much of the teachings run counter to our culture's dominant narrative about rest. As author and Episcopal priest Lauren Winner notes, we are surrounded by messages "extolling the virtues of treating yourself to a day of rest, a relaxing and leisurely visit to the spa, an extralong bubble bath, and a glass of Chardonnay." In this context, Winner asks, "Whom is the contemporary Sabbath designed to honor? . . . Why, the bubble-bath taker herself of course!" In contrast, traditional Jewish and Christian teachings on Sabbath offer an entirely different worldview. The bubble-bath taker is not at the center of the story. God is. And the gift and discipline of rest help remind us that we are not God.

After experimenting with and reading about Sabbath keeping for nearly a decade, I was excited to dive into writing this book. I wanted to share some of the experiences, challenges, and lessons I had learned along the way. And I wanted to join others who are calling for a renewed commitment to rest. We have lost something precious, as Sabbath keeping has largely faded from common life in the past half century. And I was convinced that returning to a 24/6 lifestyle could be a cure for some of what ails us as individuals, families, and a society.

Then everything changed.

I was halfway through the first draft of this book when the COVID-19 pandemic hit the world with full force. A few weeks after the first cases were reported in the United States, school districts in my state and around the country announced lengthy closures. The local and national economies skidded to a halt. The stock market crashed. The collective whiplash we experienced was both painful and frightening; most of us had never experienced anything like it before. Soon, half the world's population—more than three billion people—had been told to shelter in place.

My editor and I struggled with how I ought to proceed. I had intended to write about how living in a nonstop world affects our collective spiritual, emotional, and physical well-being. But now our world had largely stopped—or at least slowed substantially. Churches and nonessential businesses were closed. Millions of people were laid off. We couldn't travel. We couldn't eat at restaurants. We couldn't visit with friends. So what did Sabbath keeping mean in the era of COVID-19?

At the same time, the pressures at my job did not decrease. My work in international public health focuses on increasing access to maternal and reproductive health services for women in sub-Saharan Africa and Southeast Asia. As soon as the COVID-19 crisis began, we knew the pandemic would likely have devastating effects on these regions and that women and girls would be disproportionally impacted. Following other recent public health crises—including the outbreaks of Ebola, Zika, SARS, and swine flu—researchers found that these episodes "had deep, long-lasting effects on gender equality." During an epidemic, women are more likely to have to give up or reduce paid work to care for children or elders. Health-care resources are diverted from primary care, often with disastrous implications for maternal health. Rates of domestic violence and other forms of gender-based violence often rise.

Investments in global health are always important, but now our work felt even more urgent. Inaction or poor decision-making about where and how to spend time and money would have devastating consequences for people who were already incredibly vulnerable. On one hand, it didn't seem like a convenient time to be talking about the importance of rest. There was too much work to do. On the other hand, I wondered what lessons we might learn about rest, as many of us were forced to slow down.

I was not alone. During the initial days of the COVID-19 outbreak, while everyone recognized the tremendous economic and physical costs of the crisis, many also saw a potential silver lining. People asked how the crisis might create space for reevaluating our priorities and making much-needed personal and social changes.

So I made some revisions to the first half of the book and forged on with the writing, even as COVID-19 unfolded in real time. While I've included some specific reflections about the initial impact of COVID-19 in the book, ultimately many of the key takeaways remained the same. During the pandemic and during the uncertainty and anxiety of the 2020 election, I learned in new and deeper ways that I couldn't afford *not* to take a Sabbath even during—and perhaps *especially* during—a time of crisis. As the pace of life changed drastically, I found that a practice of intentional Sabbath keeping was even more relevant and necessary than before.

The first part of this book explains why I sought out a Sabbath practice in the first place. It describes some of the challenges I experienced when I first began intentionally integrating rest into my daily and weekly routines. It also describes the heartache I experienced as an eager new Christian convert who realized—after literally taking the plunge—that many Christians today do not have a daylong Sabbath observance. After six years of seeking and hoping for a communal Sabbath experience, I felt very alone and without much accountability or direction regarding how to maintain a personal and community-based Sabbath practice as a part of everyday life.

The second part of the book describes my attempts to reclaim rest, including my yearlong experiment of taking monthly Sabbath retreats. Inspired by Jesus's regular practice of withdrawing to a "solitary place" (Mark 1:35 KJV), I committed to scheduling thirty-six-hour periods away from household and work obligations each month. During that period, I also discovered unexpected moments of community within my Sabbath practice. What initially began as a deep disappointment about the lackluster approach to Sabbath I encountered in the church ultimately turned into a rich, life-affirming exploration of what rest means, how to commit to it, and how to achieve it on an ongoing basis.

The third part of the book describes my attempts to integrate Sabbath theology and practice into everyday life. This includes the period when the COVID-19 crisis dramatically changed the rhythms of work and leisure. In this part of the book, I also explore practical strategies for adopting a weekly practice of rest. A friend once said to me, "I understand what you *don't* do on the Sabbath. But what *do* you do?" This part of the book moves beyond the *why* of rest and dives more deeply into the *when* and *how*, including as one juggles work, family, household, personal health, and community service responsibilities.

The final part of the book examines in greater depth how a Sabbath ethic relates to a broader Christian theology of social justice. The violent killings of George Floyd, Breonna Taylor, and other Black Americans in the spring of 2020 as well as the disproportionate impact COVID-19 was having on communities of color contributed to what some called a "long overdue awakening" about the effects of ongoing systematic racism and violent white supremacy in the United States. As part of the process of examining and confronting the causes of widespread inequity and injustice, we must ask ourselves about the meaning, purpose, and impact of our work and our rest. Ultimately, Sabbath keeping has become a vehicle of my ongoing conversion, as I've continued to unpack and challenge the messages I received growing up about why and how we work for lasting social change and justice. Week after week, Sabbath serves as an important reminder that people cannot fix or save the world on our own; the Sabbath pierces my illusion of my self-reliance and control. Instead, I have learned in new and deeper ways how God invites us to participate in the healing and restoration of a broken world and how we must rely on God's grace in this process. The Christian story teaches us that our work is good, and rest is good. Both are part of God's vision for shalom—the promise of peace, mercy, wellbeing, and justice for all.

The book also includes a "Quick-Start Guide to Sabbath Keeping." A friend once exclaimed to me, "I know I need to read a book about rest. I just don't have time!" If you fall into this category, I encourage you to check out that section, which has several practical suggestions for incorporating rest into your life. At the same time, quick-fix strategies are not enough to transform our habits and our worldviews. Given this, exploring the *why* of rest is often as important as identifying the *when* and the *how*.

Slowly, over the past decade, the process of reclaiming rest as a spiritual discipline has transformed my life. I have discovered that while rest is certainly an effective self-care strategy, it is so much more than that. Throughout the week, I have ambitions to change the world. Like many of us, I want humanity to find and implement large-scale, effective solutions for what is broken in our institutions and systems, and I want to dedicate my life and work to contributing to these efforts. In this process, I am often tempted to worship at the altar of human effort.

Yet each Sabbath reminds us that we are not little gods. This is a hard lesson, but it is a good one. We are restless people, and we need something bigger and deeper than a temporary fix. We need more than an extralong bubble bath. In Sabbath, our ambition is challenged and our lives are transformed.

Part I

SEEKING SABBATH

1

Up in the Air

An Invitation to Slow Down

M Y MIDLIFE CRISIS BEGAN ON an airplane. We were flying home from my brother's wedding. The week we had spent in northern Vermont had been among the happiest in my life. The spot that my youngest brother, Andrew, and his fiancée, Eva, had chosen was full of meaning for all of us. The marriage ceremony took place in a hundred-year-old barn half a mile up the road from the cottage that my mother's family owned. We had visited the little town every summer since I was an infant.

The events leading up to the wedding were calm and joyful. Friends and family from all over the country trickled in during the days preceding the ceremony. Each person seemed to fall in love with the place as quickly as my husband, David, had the first summer he came to Vermont when we were still dating, almost twenty years before. Cousins tumbled into the lake, happily kayaking and eating bagel sandwiches on the small

strip of sandy beach. The adults sat in plastic lawn chairs a few
feet from the shore, drinking gin and tonics and chatting while
we watched the kids play King of the Castle on the floating
dock. The night before the wedding, we gathered for a casual
dinner at the barn. My ten-year-old daughter, Lila, and I walked
through the crowd side by side, our arms loosely wrapped
around each other's waists, her hair in two long French braids
down her back. She walked back to the cottage with my parents at bedtime while my husband and I stayed up late. We sat
in the backyard under stars untouched by city lights, laughing
with an old family friend I hadn't seen in years.

The day of the wedding was perfect. Lila, in a gauzy white
flower girl dress, walked barefoot down the aisle between the
folding chairs set out in rows beside the barn. My other brother,
Chris, stood silently by Andrew's side as his best man. Eva wore
the veil my mother had worn when she married my father forty
years before. The sideways glance and grin I saw Eva give my
brother during the ceremony spoke of love and expectation.
They seemed to share an easy joy.

Several months before the wedding, Andrew and Eva had
invited me to give the homily during the service. I had selected
a short passage from the Bible and had spent the previous six
weeks preparing my remarks. This was a new role for me. As
a newly baptized Christian, I was unaccustomed to providing
theological reflections in public. I had been raised in an agnos-
tic home; when I was a baby, my parents joined the Unitarian Universalist Church, an inclusive spiritual community that
does not adhere to any specific dogma or creed. I was raised to
be loosely "spiritual," but I hadn't had any substantial exposure to Christian thought or teachings. Then, in my twenties,
I met and married David, who had been a serious practitioner

of Buddhism since he was first introduced to the Tibetan tradition during a formative college semester in Nepal. For the first decade of our relationship, David secretly hoped I would become a Buddhist, but it didn't happen. While I admired Buddhism, it never felt like home. Yet his faith proved integral to my finding my own path. One day, when I was sitting on a meditation cushion at his Buddhist center, Jesus's presence unexpectedly washed through me. It was a dramatic conversion moment, and I was baptized a year later to the day.

Since then, I have immersed myself in Christian theology and practices. Most days I am still surprised that this is where I landed. As a young adult, hungry to find my spiritual home, I had never seriously considered Christianity as a possible path. Now I was an enthusiastic convert, continually astonished by the depth and beauty I discovered in Christian teachings. And even more surprising, in the months after my baptism, I felt a restless call to write about the journey. The memoir that resulted from that initial impulse was published the year before my brother's wedding.

So giving the homily for the ceremony that summer in Vermont still felt like a new and somewhat uncomfortable role. Most of the people at the wedding were not Christian, and I was nervous about how they would respond to my remarks.

During the ceremony, I began by expressing my gratitude to everyone for being there to demonstrate their love and support for the couple as they began a new life together. I spoke about how the land around the barn where we were gathered seems to be a "thin place," as the Celtics would say: a location where a sense of the Holy Spirit can be felt more easily than in most places. Then I read the Scripture passage I had selected: "Beloved, let us love one another, because love is from God;

everyone who loves is born of God and knows God. Whoever does not love does not know God, for God is love. . . . There is no fear in love, but perfect love casts out fear" (1 John 4:7–18). I shared that in my own life, I had experienced how marriage is often one of the best and most important places to practice loving—to begin to have God's love perfected in us. And when our imperfect love for one another inevitably fails, we must rely on God's love to shape us and strengthen us.

The rest of the ceremony went by in a rush: the vows and the kiss, the smiles and the cheering as Andrew and Eva walked hand in hand down the aisle. That night, after the ceremony and reception, we lit a huge bonfire in the field as the sun set. After an hour, everyone moved to the barn and danced for hours. The night ended with the group forming a large circle, arms slung around one another's shoulders, crooning along with Prince's "Purple Rain." Afterward, we didn't need flashlights as we walked back to our cottage in the bright moonlight.

Yes, the day and the entire week had been perfect. That's why the plane ride home was even more jarring.

◆ ◆ ◆

I made the mistake of checking my email while I was in the air. I signed on using the free internet connection the airline offered. As I scanned through the hundreds of messages I had received while I was out of the office for the week, one caught my eye. It was a note from the director of my division. She explained that one of my closest colleagues at work—a peer with whom I work closely on numerous projects—had been nominated for a prestigious award. The award was intended to recognize the outstanding work of emerging leaders under the age of forty in our field.

I looked up abruptly, and my heart rate quickened as I stared out the window. At age thirty-nine, I would have qualified for the award as well. Looking back down at my computer screen, I scanned through the rest of the emails, wondering if there had been any other nominations from our group. No. My colleague was the only one. And in that moment, I spiraled downward.

The first spiral was one of surprise and jealousy. Looking through the details, including the nomination criteria, it seemed—at least to me—that I deserved to be nominated just as much as the other woman. I had spent the last decade working relentlessly, often through late nights, weekends, and vacations. In fact, the trip to Vermont that summer was the first time I had taken a true vacation without any work in the past seven years. During my time at the large nonprofit where I worked, I'd had some notable, high-profile successes, including helping secure substantial new grant funding. The years of effort reflected a complicated mix of passionate commitment to our public health mission as well as self-serving ambition. I found the intellectual and creative challenges of the job inherently rewarding, and I also craved praise and advancement. I wanted to make the world a better place, *and* I wanted to climb the ladder of professional success. It was a mix of anxiety and fun, stress and satisfaction, service and egoism. And throughout it all, I thought my supervisors and peers recognized and appreciated my efforts. Now, in that moment, it felt as though my efforts hadn't been sufficient. I had been overlooked for this award, while my colleague, who was also a close friend, received the recognition.

When I considered the situation objectively, I suspected I knew part of the reason. My own boss had been traveling all summer, and she had probably missed the deadline, or it simply hadn't been on her radar. There was no reason to think that nominating me—or anyone else—would rise to the top of her long to-do list. And the colleague, who had been nominated by a different supervisor, was indeed a remarkable person and a fabulous contributor to our organization. Even as my jealousy flared, I acknowledged that she deserved the accolades.

And so I spiraled with a secondary pain: shame. Skimming through the congratulatory emails my colleague had received from senior leaders across the organization, I was embarrassed by the intensity of my jealousy. Not only was I arrogant in assuming that I might have been considered for the award, my envy was petty and ungenerous. I felt ashamed for caring so much either way. As a Christian, I am called to love my neighbor rather than coveting what belongs to her. I know that maintaining a heart of service and humility is what really matters. Even if my reaction on the plane was only human, I knew it was full of sin.

I knew this because, following my baptism, the teaching from Jesus that had burned most brightly for me was his claim that "the last will be first, and the first will be last" (Matthew 20:16). I found the statement both shocking and enticing. I was amazed and impressed by Jesus's assertion that he came into the world "not to be served but to serve" (Mark 10:45).

The mandate I had received my entire life—in school and at home—was that I should work to make the world a better place. But I was also surrounded by the implicit message that I should endeavor to advance my own reputation and status. There was never an explanation of how I might achieve both objectives, nor any recognition that these goals might be at odds. I had no religious framework for what it meant to be a servant leader. And I certainly hadn't looked to the teachings of Jesus for answers. When I was growing up, my mother viewed Christianity with mild antipathy. A lifelong social justice activist, she left the church of her childhood in her early twenties during the Vietnam War out of frustration with the apathy she observed from the pulpit and in the pews. Throughout my childhood, she conveyed her view that Christianity is most often a vehicle for the political right to jam sanctimonious morals and hypocritical public policies down the throat of the rest of the country. This perspective had been strongly instilled in me and my brothers. So I was shocked in my early thirties when I first explored Christian teachings to discover that the message of Jesus is actually a radical call to emptying self, loving one's neighbor, living humbly, and serving God's will instead of one's own.

As a new Christian, I deeply wanted to align myself with Jesus's transformative mandate, but—perhaps understandably—I continually found it hard to do so. And now, on the plane, awash with jealousy and hurt, I had an awareness that, spiritually, I was still at square one. In my work and daily life, I still longed for recognition and accolades, even as I tried continually to become a servant and disciple of Christ. I wanted to approach life differently, but in that moment, it was clear it wasn't working. At my most visceral level, I was unchanged, even after all my efforts at spiritual self-transformation.

Staring out of the plane's small window, I acknowledged that jealousy and shame were only a part of my reaction. Sitting there, I recognized in myself a much bigger grief. The larger sadness was that during our perfect Vermont week—a week of love and beauty, family and connection—I had let my guard down completely. I hadn't checked my email all week. I had been totally present, savoring the time with the people who are most precious to me in the place I love best in the world. And now, on the plane, I was experiencing the consequences. I felt the return to reality almost as a physical slap. The deadline for the award had passed while I was away. If I had been online or in the office, would the outcome have been different? The unspoken expectation in my workplace is that one should be online almost all the time, including on weeknights, weekends, and vacations. Over the years, I had watched colleagues get overlooked for opportunities for new projects when they were out of the office on leave and perceived as unavailable, even for just a week or two. Vigilance, both in protecting one's turf and in jockeying for recognition, seemed crucial.

Sitting in the narrow seat, I wanted to cry. In that moment, being overlooked for the award felt like a tangible, painful consequence of choosing to unplug. Yet I didn't want to think this way; I didn't want to be this person. I didn't want to live that kind of life.

◆ ◆ ◆

I was born at the tail end of the 1970s, which makes me part of Generation X. In her recent book *Why We Can't Sleep: Women's New Midlife Crisis*, author Ada Calhoun provides compelling evidence that Gen X women in the United States, who are now in midlife, are experiencing a silent epidemic of low-grade but persistent misery. Calhoun points to the data. Among American women in middle age, one in four takes an antidepressant. Almost 60 percent describe themselves as stressed, and three-quarters say they are worried about money. Part of this anxiety is due to the pressures we put on ourselves. Calhoun aptly writes, "For this generation of women, the belief that girls could do anything morphed into a directive that they must do everything." At the same time, the external stressors experienced at home and at work are very real. Women in midlife often "bear financial responsibilities that men had in the old days while still saddled with traditional caregiving duties." And women "generally incur this double whammy precisely while hitting peak stress in both . . . careers and child-raising." Simultaneously, the financial pressures on families have increased; many families today are "downwardly mobile, with declining job stability." All of this has happened just as the pace and volume of communication have sped up. Calhoun says, "We are bombarded with catastrophic breaking news alerts, social media's curated images of others' success, and nonstop work obligations—not to mention phone calls, texts and email." The result is that "our lives can begin to feel like the latter seconds of a game of Tetris, where the descending pieces pile up faster and faster."

Calhoun puts the anxiety that many in my generation experience within a historical context. As a kid, I grew up during the final decades of the Cold War; my mother later told me that in the 1980s, she worried that my brothers and I might not have the chance to grow up because of the possibility of a nuclear holocaust. As teenagers, my peers and I lived through the emergence of the HIV/AIDS epidemic. As I began dating, the main message I received was that sex could kill you. When I was a freshman in high school, the police officers who had violently beaten Rodney King in Los Angeles were acquitted, and six days of rioting broke out across the city. During that spring, racial tensions in my own high school ran high. I grew up in an affluent community outside of Boston that has participated in a decades-long school desegregation initiative, through which low-income students from predominantly Black and Latino neighborhoods in Boston are bused each day to mostly white suburbs to attend public school. During the first semester of my freshman year, I was sitting in gym class when a group of white and Black girls began fighting; the incident began when one of the girls stood up and spat in the face of the other. As a fourteen-year-old, I struggled to understand what was happening. Calhoun made me realize my experience was not uncommon. She writes, "There was a stark contrast between what we were taught (racism was defeated by the Freedom Riders) and what we witnessed (rampant racism in society, racial tension in our schools). Yet . . . there was no reckoning with the distance between our parents' ideals and our reality."

Like many in my generation, I was raised to believe it was my job to help make the world a better place. As a result, I've spent many years wondering what my role should be in trying to address systematic injustice. Yet throughout my life, while I've recognized the impact of widespread oppression and violence, I've often felt helpless in knowing how to respond.

As I neared my fortieth birthday, I continued to struggle with these questions. Across almost every dimension, things in my life were going well. I had a wonderful family, savings in my bank account, relatively good health, a strong church community, and despite the challenges, a job I loved. Yet I was chronically stressed out. During the year before my brother's wedding, I had begun waking up at three o'clock every morning, my mind racing. I worried about my own life, and I worried about the world. I started taking a short-acting anxiety medication, at first occasionally and then more frequently, so I could sleep, and then I finally switched to a daily dose of a selective serotonin reuptake inhibitor to "take the edge off."

It had worked to a degree; I was sleeping better. But I was still often overwhelmed and exhausted, and I wondered if I needed to make other, more substantial changes in my life.

In that moment up in the sky, flying home from my brother's wedding, I recognized that the intensity of my reaction to my friend's nomination for the award was a wake-up call. My jealousy of a colleague's success, my inability to trust that my reputation would be intact when I got back from a much-needed break, my confusion about how to advance my career while making a lasting difference in the world, my growing generalized anxiety: all of this indicated I needed to make a change.

The plane descended, and the wheels bumped hard as we landed on the runway, jostling us all in our seats. The plane seemed to be going faster than normal, and the woman behind me let out a small cry. I gripped David's arm, digging my nails into his forearm. The pilot must have pumped the brakes, because we decelerated with a rapid hiss. The wheels swerved slightly, and we all lurched forward in our seats. The plane stopped abruptly, and the passengers looked at one another, both relieved and unnerved.

Glancing around the aisles, I got the message. We all needed to slow down.

2

Anorexia of the Soul

The Dangers of an Overscheduled Life

WHEN I WAS A YOUNG adult, the Sunday edition of the *New York Times* ran a cover story about the high school I had attended. The story was entitled "For Girls, It's Be Yourself, and Be Perfect, Too," and it described the intense pressure students feel to do it all, even at a young age. Most students are expected to build flawless résumés reflecting academic success and a diverse mix of extracurricular activities, leadership roles, and community service. And while parents want their children to be high achieving, they also want them to be down-to-earth; teens are advised to combat stress by striving for "balance" in their lives. The writer noted that the pressure seems particularly intense for girls. Girls are expected (and expect themselves) to be smart, successful, fun, and "effortlessly hot." The commercial area near the high school reflects the complicated, often conflicting messages the kids receive. There are expensive SAT test prep services, after-school tutoring programs, multiple psychotherapists' offices, and several yoga studios promising physical wellness and inner peace.

The author concluded, "There is something about the lives these girls lead—their jam-packed schedules, the amped-up multitasking . . . that speaks of a profound anxiety in the young people, but perhaps even more so in their parents." One of the parents interviewed recognized the risk involved with the lifestyle; the mother said she worried that young people will develop "anorexia of the soul."

Reading the article in my twenties, I found it deeply validating. As a sophomore at the public school described in the article, I had developed a consuming panic disorder that plagued me off and on throughout high school and college. Outwardly, I excelled. I served as the editor in chief of my high school literary magazine and got accepted into a prestigious liberal arts college. I went on to graduate from college with honors in three and a half years of classes. I had a large circle of friends and a couple of serious boyfriends. I was fun and (I hoped) effortlessly hot.

But by the time I reached my senior year of college—facing an uncertain and unknowable future and losing the security of a close-knit community—I felt like I was falling off a cliff. By then, I had been in therapy for nearly a third of my life; I had started going to weekly counseling sessions when I was fifteen. Therapy seemed to help, but then, during each period of major transition, I would find myself in crisis again. For months during the spring semester of my senior year, I experienced daily panic attacks. I lost twenty pounds because I gagged every time I tried to eat. I was miserable, and I hated feeling that way. I didn't know the solution, but I wanted to change my life.

The modern era has frequently been referred to as the "age of anxiety." People of all backgrounds and incomes—not just privileged, overachieving kids in the United States—seem to be affected. Anxiety disorders are the most prevalent types of mental health disorders globally, according to the World Health Organization. Social scientists, psychologists, economists, and theologians have posited a number of theories about the reasons for this trend: erosion of community, separation from family and nature, a rise of consumerism, rapid urbanization, growing secularism and existential alienation, sedentary lifestyles, too much screen time. A disconnection from self, others, and God. All of the above.

After college, I moved to a farm in rural North Carolina, where I lived for several years in a little cabin and worked part-time. The time there was deeply healing. It allowed me to unwind, spend time in nature, engage in physical labor, and form community with people who had intentionally stepped off the fast track. Most importantly, the time at the farm helped me reorient my values in subtle but important ways. By the time I went back to graduate school, got married, and started a career and family, I had changed many of my habits, and I had new role models.

But then, as a young professional and working mother, I experienced the return of a familiar pattern. External and internalized expectations dictated that I achieve both success and balance, which seemed like an elusive, if not impossible, task. And there was another challenge. Unlike in the 1990s when I was in high school and college, cell phones and social media had become ubiquitous. A massive proliferation and acceleration of communication had occurred, and there seemed to be no boundaries when it came to work and time off. In my job, colleagues responded to emails late at night and throughout the weekends. Supervisors worked through vacations and holidays;

one year, our project director wrote our team an email on Thanksgiving morning.

Experts refer to this phenomenon as "job creep." In an article in the *Wall Street Journal* entitled "Sunday Night Is the New Monday Morning, and Workers Are Miserable," reporter Kelsey Gee writes that while some industries are experimenting with "structured disengagement strategies" such as email bans during weekends or when employees are on vacation, it is "no longer practical for many employers to set hard limits on when staff should be reachable, since business is being conducted around the clock, often by colleagues across the globe." This is true in my own organization; we have offices in over sixty countries around the world, and most of us work on projects that span several time zones.

But the lifestyle was increasingly exhausting. Like many others, I was juggling the demands of work, a young family, a long commute, and an ongoing desire to make a real impact in the world. Being hot no longer felt effortless. I needed exercise and sleep. But I didn't want to return to the type of lifestyle I cultivated at the farm as a young woman; I loved my career and my family. I wanted it all. But I also knew I was at risk of anorexia of the soul.

I felt like I was spiraling until a friend posed a surprising question: she asked if I had ever considered a Sabbath practice.

3

///

Sabbath Neuroses

Experimentations with Rest

I WAS FIRST EXPOSED TO THE idea of Sabbath keeping several years before I converted to Christianity. A friend and mentor had given me a copy of Wayne Muller's book *Sabbath*. The concepts and insights felt revelatory. Muller writes, "The ancient rabbis teach that on the seventh day, God created *menuha*—tranquility, serenity, peace and repose. . . . Until the Sabbath, creation was unfinished." In Hebrew, *menuha* means more than a respite from work; it is a deep delight in rest. And without Sabbath time, the rabbis taught, the world is incomplete.

Reading this, my stress and confusion suddenly made sense. No wonder so many of us are exhausted, anxious, and broken in our inner and outer lives. We have turned our backs on a critical, beautiful, intrinsic part of creation and our humanity: rest. And, Muller argues, the way to start reclaiming this birthright is shockingly easy and rooted in millennia of tradition: abstaining from work one day a week and creating space to allow menuha to return to one's life. As I read more, a Sabbath observance sounded straightforward, intuitive, and potentially life changing.

In some ways, it was surprising I hadn't been exposed to Sabbath keeping earlier in my life because the community where I grew up outside of Boston was largely Jewish. But while most of my friends' families identified as culturally Jewish, many were not particularly religious. They celebrated high holidays; as a teenager, I was invited as a guest to several Passover Seders. But I didn't know anyone who had a committed, weekly Shabbat observance. As a young adult, I was largely ignorant of what Sabbath keeping entailed in practice for most observant Jews or Christians.

At the time, I was in a period of spiritual exploration, so I decided to make up a Sabbath practice of my own. I didn't have any formal guidance, but I would use common sense and do what felt right. I committed to setting aside twenty-four hours each week for rest. Since I wasn't Jewish and I still often went to Unitarian Universalist Church services on Sunday mornings, I decided to observe the Sabbath on Sundays. The rules I adopted were no chores, no email, no errands, no social media, no to-do lists. At the beginning, I convinced my husband and kids to try it with me, and the time we set aside each week without work felt deeply restorative. The best days were when my teenage stepson, Soren, participated. One Sunday we sat on the back porch together all afternoon. It was a beautiful, warm day, and amazingly, everyone agreed to put away their devices without too much of a fuss. In the hours that followed, we chatted. We laughed. We snacked. We read. We cleaned the pine needles off our largely unused outdoor ping pong table, and David beat Soren three games in a row. It was fun and deeply relaxing.

But then my family started to balk. The kids complained that they had homework to finish, and David said he didn't want to be told what he could and couldn't do on his day off. As a Buddhist, David said that Sabbath keeping wasn't part of his religious tradition, and he didn't want to be constrained by arbitrary rules. If he wanted and needed to mow the lawn on a Sunday, he would do it. We started to bicker. I asserted that for me, this was about something much bigger. For years, David had been admonishing me to slow down, to stop multitasking, to make changes in my life so I would be less stressed out. He said that my amped-up pace was affecting the entire family. A shared day of family Sabbath time could be the answer, I pointed out. It seemed obvious to me; this was a solution through which we could find common ground. Wasn't this just what he had been asking me to do all along?

No, he said; he had a different idea. He wanted me to pace myself throughout the workweek. He personally had no desire to work at a breakneck speed. He didn't think the solution was to work manically all week and then collapse for one day. He wanted us to move more slowly all week long. I bristled at this idea. I was attracted to working at maximum capacity: pushing myself to the limit of what I was capable of and then, afterward, resting deeply. Moving fast rather than at a plodding pace allowed me to achieve more. I liked the adrenaline, and I liked being highly productive. And then, when my energy flagged, the antidote would be a regular discipline of rest. The logic made sense to me, but it didn't make sense to David.

So even though I longed for a shared family experience, and even though maintaining a Sabbath practice alone felt less appealing, I persevered on my own. The kids did homework on Sundays, and David did chores, but I completed all of my tasks on Saturday. I would finish the weekly grocery shopping and my other chores by Saturday night. And then I would stop. I would stay off social media, leave any piles of laundry and other messes around the house untouched, and abstain from running errands. The practice felt lonely sometimes but also deeply gratifying. I wasn't always successful in having pristine boundaries, particularly in relation to checking my work email. But I tried. One week, restless to end my Sabbath observance an hour early so I could send a quick email to a colleague, I forced myself to take a walk instead. The evening sky above my street was streaked with purple and lined with golden clouds. I knew that without the Sabbath, I never would have looked up.

In those months, the Sabbath became one of my best teachers. The weekly observance began to challenge my belief that we create and achieve entirely on our own. I realized the extent to which I deified human effort; I had been raised to believe that people can save themselves if they just work hard enough. As I kept up with my regular practice of Sabbath keeping, I began to question my long-held belief that human redemption is something we can work out entirely on our own. The Sabbath also helped me confront my assumption that there are no limits on what I could or should be doing. Perhaps the constraints I experienced were just as important as the opportunities.

The Sabbath also became one of my most difficult teachers. I was surprised that on many Sundays, I would often feel unsettled. All the anxiety I had managed to keep at bay during the week seemed to catch up with me on that day. As I read more, I learned the reaction is commonplace. One of Freud's students, Sandor Ferenczi, observed a pattern of increased complaints of psychosomatic symptoms on the Sabbath; he coined the phrase *Sunday neurosis*. Likewise, Viktor Frankl wrote in his book *Man's Search for Meaning* that this anxiety "afflicts people who become aware of the lack of content in their lives when the rush of the busy week is over and the void within themselves becomes manifest." Although not always comfortable, the unsettling moments I experienced during the Sabbath seemed important to acknowledge and experience. I wanted to pay attention to what happened when I stopped all activity and striving.

Despite the rich experience I was having with Sabbath keeping, over time I struggled to maintain the weekly practice. I started to relax my own rules and end my Sabbath by midafternoon on Sundays so I could turn back to my long and weighty to-do lists. In those moments, I knew I couldn't do it alone. I needed community. And I still wasn't clear about the when, where, and how of Sabbath keeping.

I wondered if I should observe the Sabbath from Saturday sundown to Sunday sundown or through Sunday night as well. Without formal rituals to open and close Sabbath, like there are in Judaism, how could I mark the beginning and ending of the holy time? What activities should be "in" and "out" on the Sabbath? Making the rules up on my own no longer felt adequate. I was eager for structure, support, and accountability.

So a few years later, when Jesus unexpectedly showed up in my life and called me to him, I was excited about what becoming a Christian would mean for my Sabbath practice. I would finally have role models and concrete guidelines. Even if my Buddhist husband didn't want to observe the Sabbath with me, I would find companions at church. The desire for a shared Sabbath observance wasn't the initial impetus for my conversion, but it seemed like a fabulous side benefit. I was thrilled to think the church could help me reclaim the gift of rest.

4

///

Sabbath Ambivalence

From Church to Mall

S TANDING IN COFFEE HOUR after the church service, I
felt my muscles tighten as other parishioners shared their
afternoon plans and said their goodbyes.

"Come on, Jennifer. We need to go to the mall to get you a
new pair of shoes."

"I'm heading home now to grade papers this afternoon."

"Well, I'm off to the grocery store. Have a great week!"

A year into my life as a newly baptized Christian, I was
disheartened to realize that almost no one at church seemed to
have an intentional Sabbath practice. After the worship service
was over, it seemed like Sundays were generally treated like any
other day.

When I became a Christian, I didn't think I was particularly naive. My eyes were wide open about the destructive ways
that many Christians had wielded their religion over centuries
and in many different contexts. And I knew the contemporary

church was far from perfect. Despite this, I felt a nascent but blossoming relationship with God, and I was slowly getting to know Jesus. When I read Christian teachings, I was overwhelmed by their beauty and mystery, and I felt challenged by their radical invitation to self-emptying love. In contrast to the Christians I read about in the news, the Christians I knew in person were generally kind, humble, and quietly faithful. Many were social justice warriors whose faith buoyed and strengthened their activism and service. Overall, my entry into the church felt like a profound and joyous homecoming.

Once the honeymoon period faded, however, I knew enough to be prepared to experience disappointments in the church. But in the first year after my baptism, there hadn't been any scandals, insurmountable theological conundrums, or difficult congregational dynamics. Instead, my biggest surprise and sorrow was that I still felt alone in my Sabbath keeping.

In addition to being lonely, I was confused. During the worship service each week, the congregation would kneel together in prayer and recite the Decalogue. "Remember the Sabbath day, and keep it holy," the priest would announce. "Amen. Lord have mercy," we responded each week in unison. I didn't understand. Didn't anyone else see the disconnect? It was clear from casual conversation that many parishioners were serious about maintaining a variety of dedicated spiritual disciplines. People casually referenced their daily prayer practices and regular Bible study. The Eucharist was revered, and I knew a number of people who met periodically with one of the priests for confession. As a parish, we were invited to adopt various liturgical practices throughout the church year, including during Lent and Advent. People at church seemed to have gusto for all of this.

But when it came to Sabbath keeping, the sentiment seemed different. At most, people seemed to think that Sabbath was synonymous with the hour-long worship service we attended on Sunday mornings. But I kept wondering, Doesn't the Sabbath described in the Bible last longer than an hour or two? When we knelt together in prayer, hadn't we asked for God's help to keep the entire *day* holy?

In his best-selling book *Celebration of Discipline*, author Richard Foster makes the case that rather than constraining or oppressing us, rigorous spiritual disciplines can "bring freedom." I agreed. As an earnest new convert who had grown up in an "anything goes" religious culture, I didn't want to be on a pick-and-choose spiritual path anymore. Part of the attraction of a committed religious life is having a structured doctrine that forces us to bang up against the edges of what feels comfortable and easy. When it came to Sabbath keeping, I wanted the constraints that came with a prescribed, time-bound, weekly discipline. And I wanted to observe the practice in the context of community.

Part of me felt silly for being so disappointed. What did it matter if other churchgoers included a daylong Sabbath observance in their spiritual repertoire? It wasn't as if people were saying cheerfully at coffee hour, "Well, I'm off to sleep with my friend's wife this afternoon!"

Still, didn't our communal prayer suggest that observing the Sabbath is just as much a commandment as the prohibition against adultery? Beyond my growing theological confusion about whether Sabbath keeping is an "official" Christian discipline, my disappointment was deeply personal. I was still struggling to find that elusive balance, the balance that I had been told for so long I ought to strive to achieve. I knew that compulsive work—especially when intertwined with a desire for external accolades—can quickly become pathological. Yet underfunctioning to obtain a calm, hassle-free lifestyle also seemed problematic. The latter approach seemed to contradict the feminist messages I had received growing up: that I ought to live up to my potential as an educated young woman with unprecedented opportunities. And now I had a Christian understanding of vocation as well. I knew God was calling me to contribute in the world and use my gifts in a myriad of ways. I wanted both meaningful work and deep rest. But it was hard to achieve both, especially in a world where the boundaries between work and rest were increasingly porous.

Given these challenges, I wanted my church to provide the tools and framework so that finally, with God's help, I could hopefully move toward a balanced life. I had taken the plunge, literally, when I had been baptized. Now I wanted my church to live up to my expectations.

◆ ◆ ◆

My husband, David, is a clinical psychologist, and after being married to him for fifteen years, I have learned a few tricks of his trade. I've learned that when it comes to making people feel better, the four most powerful words often are "Your feelings make sense." This affirmation does not mean that the world ought to change in response to our feelings (contrary to what most of us think we want). But even if the external world doesn't change much, it helps to have someone tell us that, given our unique needs, circumstances, interpretations, and desires, our feelings make sense.

A big, sulky part of me wanted that kind of validation regarding the Sabbath. I felt whiny and petulant. I wanted someone to affirm my intense and unrelenting desire for a communal Sabbath experience. I wanted to know I wasn't crazy for being confused and disappointed by the apathetic reaction to Sabbath I had encountered in the church. I wanted someone to tell me that my feelings made sense.

Judith Shulevitz's book *The Sabbath World* finally offered the validation I was seeking. Shulevitz responded to her own deep yearning for and conflicted feelings about Sabbath by diving deeply into the history of Sabbath keeping and its meaning for both Jews and Christians. Since the beginning, Christians have had ambivalent feelings about the Sabbath. First of all, the theology of Sabbath keeping has been confusing for many, particularly in light of Paul's teachings that through Christ's death and resurrection, we now transcend the law. Beyond this, people's conflicted attitudes are particularly pronounced in the United States, given our unique historical relationship with the Sabbath. Shulevitz writes,

> Americans, once the most Sabbatarian people on earth, are now the most ambivalent on the subject. On one hand, we miss the Sabbath. When we pine for escape from the rat race; when we check into spas, yoga centers, encounter weekends, spiritual retreats . . . we are remembering the Sabbath, its power to protect us from our own desires. But when . . . we feel a sense of relief that our twenty-four hour economy allows us to work, shop, dine, and be entertained when *we* want to, not according to some imposed schedule, at that point, too, we are remembering the Sabbath. We are remembering how claustrophobic its rigid temporal boundaries used to feel.

Shulevitz gives a historical context for our schizophrenic relationship with Sabbath keeping. In colonial New England in the 1600s, the Puritans were fanatical about the Sabbath. In some ways, the Puritans had the kind of communal structure I was seeking; they stopped work on Saturday afternoons so that they could prepare their homes and hearts, and Sundays were spent in worship, self-reflection, penitence, and acts of charity for the poor. They exalted the Sabbath both as part of God's natural created order and as one of the most import-ant components of living a holy and sanctified life. However, the Puritans' version of Sabbath keeping was both austere and draconian. The Massachusetts colony enacted *The Book of General Law and Liberties* in 1647, which made church atten-dance compulsory and penalized acts of Sabbath breaking—including socializing, frivolity, and traveling—with fines and other punishments. A friend of mine from church sent me a notice she had discovered when she was studying her family history. On October 3, 1662, in Barnstable, Massachusetts, her ancestor had been "fined 10 shillings for riding a journey on the Lord's day."

During the Puritans' heyday, Shulevitz explains, the imposed rigor did not mean that the day was without spiritual richness. For the Puritans, the Sabbath was meant to "crackle with high drama and sensual joy." However, "all these things happened inside the soul, not out in the world." So outwardly, Sundays were not much fun. Puritans spent most of the day in church in unheated meetinghouses, and people were punished if they were caught doing things like laundry or walking down the road with a sweetheart. The regulations in New England became informally known as the "blue laws," and even during the early years, they were controversial, with various groups challenging them on both theological and legal grounds. None-theless, Puritan-inspired norms regarding Sabbath keeping became enshrined in American law and culture. In many states, versions of blue laws stayed on the books until the late twentieth century, with some still remaining intact. In North Carolina, where I live, alcohol cannot be purchased until noon on Sundays (unless municipalities vote to change it to ten o'clock according to a new "brunch bill"), and liquor stores must remain closed all day.

Beyond the legal considerations, Puritan-inspired cultural norms were oppressive for many. When Maria von Trapp, made famous by her portrayal in *The Sound of Music*, moved to the United States, she was shocked that American Sabbath keeping lacked the "serenity and peace" of Sundays in her homeland of Austria. She wrote,

> The climax of our discoveries about the American Sunday was reached when a lady exclaimed to us with real feeling, "Oh, how I hate Sunday! What a bore! . . . I was brought up the Puritan way. Every Saturday night our mother used to collect all our toys and lock them up. On Sunday morning we children had to sit through a long sermon which we didn't understand; we were not allowed to jump or run or play. . . . We could sit on the front porch with the grownups or read the Bible. That was the only book allowed on Sunday. . . . Oh, how I hated Sunday when I was young. I vowed to myself that when I grew up I would do the dirtiest work on Sunday, and if I should have children, they would be allowed to do exactly as they pleased. They wouldn't even have to go to church."

This sentiment was echoed by Christians I spoke to who had grown up observing the Sabbath. Some had happy memories of shared meals and leisurely family time, but others remember stifling tedium. A friend who is in her seventies explained that during her childhood in the rural Midwest, the Sabbath could be pleasant, with large family gatherings each Sunday afternoon. But over time, her parents' generation began to balk. The men didn't want to wear suits all day, and the women wanted to play cards. As the complaints continued and escalated over time, my friend's grandmother eventually gave in, and Sabbath keeping was abandoned as a family tradition.

Given this complicated history, the ambivalence I perceived among other churchgoers about Sabbath keeping began to make sense. While my yearning for Sabbath rest was valid, the resistance others felt was legitimate too. I might crave discipline and structure, but nobody wanted to revert to legalism. Given this, there was no easy solution to the Sabbath conundrum I faced. I wanted to observe the Sabbath in the context of community, but my community was lukewarm about the idea. My feelings made sense, but theirs did too.

Perhaps it was time for a collective "refresh" of Sabbath practices. In their highly acclaimed book *Resident Aliens*, theologians Stanley Hauerwas and William Willimon make the dramatic claim that Christendom died in America during their childhoods when movie theaters started opening on Sundays. For the first time, in the mid-1960s, a person could freely choose between church and secular culture. While some Christians today perceive this as a loss, the authors argue that this actually creates an important opportunity. Untangling religion from capitalism allows Jesus's followers to shape their lives more fully around their discipleship. A deeper, more authentic Christianity becomes possible.

Given this, I wondered if we could start to shed the complicated history and baggage around Sabbath keeping and embrace a reimagined Sabbath. As a first step, I knew I needed to understand what Jesus himself had to say about the Sabbath. Jesus tells us, "The Son of man is Lord even of the sabbath" (Matthew 12:8 KJV). But what does this mean in practice? I needed to better grasp the theology, and I had to keep looking for community in my Sabbath keeping.

❖ ❖ ❖

I finally found a role model when I read J. Dana Trent's book *For Sabbath's Sake*. As part of her research, Trent interviewed dozens of clergy members about their own Sabbath practices. She found that while many church pastors aspire to a dedicated Sabbath observance, most find it challenging. Trent writes that for the majority of clergy, "insisting on and modeling the six-and-one rhythm of stopping, ceasing, praising and serving escapes their grasp." Church staff must work on Sundays, of course, and while they often try to designate another day for a full- or half-day Sabbath observance, in reality, "they struggle to protect that time." The result is that "clergy Sabbath is rare; committee meetings pop up, emergencies arise, and ministers feel that they are on call for their flock 24/7, especially if their churches are short-staffed."

But in her interviews, Trent spoke to someone who was an exception. When she interviewed Rev. Vanna Fox, a pastor in North Carolina, Fox explained that in addition to a weekly Sabbath practice, she sets aside time each month for an extended Sabbath retreat. Her rules are no talking, no other people, no phones, and no internet for thirty-six hours. The time is reserved for quiet reflection, fasting, prayer, and rest. Rev. Fox's retreats are clearly rooted in Scripture. Not only was Jesus an observant Sabbatarian, he consistently modeled the importance of periodically withdrawing to a "deserted place" (Mark 1:35) for silence, solitude, and prayer. Like Jesus, Trent concluded, we should regularly set aside periods of time for quiet, reflection, and being alone. A weekly Sabbath practice should not be the only time we reserve for rest.

I loved the idea, but I wasn't sure how to implement something like that in practice, given everything I had going on. I didn't know if or how I could negotiate time away from my family and work. But the idea of taking intentional monthly retreats stayed with me. I had reached a level of exhaustion that almost frightened me. I knew something had to change; I couldn't sustain my current pace. I wasn't sure how, but I would make it work. I would take a Sabbath year.

Part II

A SABBATH YEAR

5

///

Itchy Birds

The Real Meaning of Mindfulness

B EFORE I STARTED MY YEAR of Sabbath retreats, I told a friend about my plan. She was enthusiastic and—I could hear in her voice—a bit envious. "I love the idea," she said. "But where are you going to do it?" I was surprised by the question. Of all the challenges, the *where* seemed the least daunting. It was the how and the when that worried me. Even if David agreed, how could I take time away without feeling guilty? When would I be able to squeeze something else into my already overpacked schedule?

As I predicted, the where worked out fairly easily the first month. A close friend was out of town, and I asked if I could stay in her condo. She didn't have any pets and barely any plants, so she didn't need a house sitter, but she said it was no problem to use her space. After some negotiation, I resolved the *when* question as well. I requested a Friday off from work so that our already limited family time on the weekends wouldn't be affected too much. My daughter would be at school all day, and David would greet her when she got off the bus. My stepson was with his mom that weekend. I left after dinner on Thursday, and we agreed I would return home Saturday morning. In the meantime, I was free for thirty-six hours.

I arrived at my friend's apartment at around eight o'clock in the evening. The silence felt both strange and spacious. Lying in bed between my friend's white cotton sheets, I felt both vaguely unsettled and quietly delighted. What would this solitude hold? I looked around the room and felt the emptiness of the time ahead of me. My head and neck felt heavy, and I realized how tired I was. I fell asleep early, with the light still on.

The next morning I made myself a simple breakfast. In my hurried preparation the night before, I had packed a plastic container with two uncooked eggs, an avocado, and half a tomato from our refrigerator. I drizzled oil into a pan I found in my friend's cupboard and held one of the eggs in my hand, pausing to feel its surface in my palm. Cracking it sharply against the pan's edge, I watched as the translucent liquid slid against the hot surface and turned white almost instantly. I dropped in several tomato slices, and they sizzled beside the eggs. After the edges of the tomato darkened and the egg yolk felt hot to the touch, I slid them onto a plate and spooned the avocado on top, pinching salt out of a small bowl on the windowsill. I ate at my friend's kitchen table, unsure if I was lonely or relieved or just unaccustomed to the silence.

After breakfast, I put on my sneakers. I never have enough time to exercise, so I figured I would begin my miniretreat with a jog. But when I got out to the sidewalk, my body felt heavy, and I found myself swaying slightly. I realized I was too tired to run. Impulsively, I sat down where I was standing, right in the middle of the sidewalk. I knew I must have looked strange, but I figured that since this retreat was partly about stopping all effort and activity, I could do so with a bit of dramatic flair.

For the next forty-five minutes, I sat on the sidewalk, not moving. After about twenty minutes, a woman in the condo next door stuck her head out of the window and asked if I was all right. I reassured her with a smile and wave, saying, "Just resting. I'll move in a little bit."

"OK." She nodded, pulling her head back inside the window. I rotated out toward the street and scooted forward a bit, my sneakered feet resting on the curb. It was a quiet neighborhood, with no other pedestrians and only a few cars. There wasn't much to look at, but oddly, I felt no inclination to move.

Across the street, I noticed a small gray bird sitting at the top of a telephone pole. I am not a birdwatcher; my few attempts at maintaining a backyard birdfeeder have failed under the constant onslaught of squirrels. As I sat there, I watched the bird scratching its body. He was relentless. Over and over, the bird dug at his chest and sides with his beak, ruffling and then smoothing down his feathers. A few seconds later, he would start again, pushing his beak deep beneath his wings, chasing some unknown irritant. Watching the bird scratch himself didn't feel particularly glamorous. It wasn't a transcendent moment. Still, I wondered if the bird was a spiritual metaphor. Perhaps the point of my time away was to become more mindful of the little bird on the pole. Maybe he was an envoy from God as I began my retreat. Then again, maybe he was just incredibly itchy.

I have complicated feelings about the concept of mindfulness and its growing popularity. As Americans increasingly acknowledge their exhaustion, anxiety, and distractibility, they are seeking new tools for finding rest and restoration. In the

United States, there is growing interest in mindfulness meditation as a health improvement strategy, a spiritual practice, and an overall framework for life. Increasingly, messages in our popular culture support this. We are enjoined to eat mindfully, wash dishes mindfully, and parent with mindfulness. Classes in mindfulness meditation are now commonly offered in hospitals, schools, and prisons; by human resource departments and sports teams; and even within the US military. Numerous apps, such as Headspace and Calm, help users implement mindfulness practices. For me, this feels confusing. Is the implication that all our experiences, however banal, should be observed with a mixture of attentiveness, detachment, and appreciation? At its heart, what is the goal of all this mindfulness?

◆ ◆ ◆

I'm not alone in wondering about the meaning and impact of our hyperfocus on mindful living. Author Ruth Whippman points out that the call for greater mindfulness "often contains a hefty scoop of moralizing smugness, a kind of 'moment-shaming' for the distractible." Increasingly, a secularized version of mindfulness is being co-opted by a capitalist agenda, she says, with Americans now spending an estimated $4 billion a year on mindfulness products.

Also, current mindfulness strategies are laced with problematic messages, Whippman argues. In the workforce, mindfulness training has become just another strategy to increase employees' productivity. In schools, mindfulness initiatives can gloss over damaging structural inequities in our education system. And at home, mindful parenting can lead to overindulgence of already coddled kids. "Mindfulness is supposed to be a defense against the pressures of modern life, but it's starting to feel suspiciously like it's actually adding to them," writes Whippman. "It's a special circle of self-improvement hell, striving not just for a Pinterest-worthy home, but a Pinterest-worthy mind."

I have had many discussions about mindfulness with my husband, David, who has been a serious Buddhist practitioner for twenty-five years and a teacher for ten. David agrees that contemporary portrayals of mindfulness in mainstream American culture are often a distortion of traditional Buddhist teachings. Contrary to popular conceptions, mindfulness practices in Buddhism are not primarily intended to help us be more "present" to our surroundings and experiences per se but rather are meant to help us live more virtuous lives. Buddhist practitioners believe it is critical to train the mind to increase focus, but ultimately, that is just a preparatory step. Once the mind is less distracted, the student can reflect on, absorb, and incorporate Buddhist teachings on how we can reduce our self-cherishing and cultivate greater compassion and virtue. It's not that mindfulness is unimportant; it is just that secularized versions miss the larger point.

Rather than an attempt to control the mind to achieve worldly goals, mindfulness in Buddhism helps cultivate awareness to develop insight into the true nature of the mind. These more nuanced teachings on mindfulness are more difficult—and less popular—than the promise of a stress-free, "be here now" mental zone. As such, those messages typically don't make it onto coffee mugs or Facebook memes.

Likewise, in Christianity, meditation and contemplative prayer emphasize the importance of interior silence, but this, too, is a means to an end. The Latin word *meditatio* means both "to contemplate" and "to rehearse." In Christian meditation, you quietly think something over to prepare for something else. Whether you're repeating a short prayer phrase, engaged in the ancient practice of *lectio divina* (holy reading) to reflect deeply on a Scripture verse, silently observing your breath, or using prayer beads, the ultimate goal is to prepare yourself to enter into a deeper communion with God. As author Carl McColman points out, meditation is *relational*. As we quiet our minds and bodies, the "goal is not so much about mastering silence or achieving a desired state of consciousness"; rather, "it is the relational act of responding to, seeking, and nurturing intimacy with God."

But how do we do this? Our lives are so busy, noisy, outwardly oriented, and technology filled that we have no idea how to cultivate a body and mind of stillness so we can be more open to listening for God. Richard Foster writes, "If we are constantly being swept off our feet with frantic activity, we will be unable to be attentive at the moment of inward silence." This is part of why we have to create time for solitude, rest, meditation, and prayer.

The call for a balanced, measured pace is not just a response to the stresses and demands of modernity. The early church fathers wrote about *otium sanctum*, or "holy leisure." This, Foster explains, "refers to a sense of balance in the life . . . an ability to rest and take time to enjoy beauty. An ability to pace ourselves." This was exactly what was missing in my life: an ability to pace myself. I embrace a frantic lifestyle, even as I know that kind of internal and external rhythm leaves me enervated and irritable, requiring medication to sleep. Too often I want to maximize my productivity and impact in the world, but I rarely ask myself if I want to maximize my relationship with God. Sadly, when I am honest with myself, I am not sure which is more important to me.

Maybe that's why I was sitting there on the curb watching a bird scratch its wings. The itchy bird was an invitation into mindfulness but for different reasons than those typically offered in our popular culture. The goal wasn't to lock the bird down in my mindfulness memory bank with detached appreciation. Nor was it to reduce my stress level to help me recover from—and ultimately sustain—a hectic, multitasking lifestyle. Instead, the moment of sitting still became a moment of holy leisure and, in turn, a time of holy preparation.

As I watched myself watching the bird, what I noticed most was my self-referential habits. I had started off by wondering if the bird was a spiritual harbinger—if his presence held some sort of secret message for me that I needed to decode. But if there was any message, it was an invitation to pay attention to what was actually going on in the world rather than what I superimposed upon it. In truth, the bird had nothing to do with me; remarkably, I am not the reference point of the universe. Instead, if I paid attention to a small, itchy bird nearby, maybe I would become better at paying attention to the other ways God is showing up in the world. Perhaps I would slowly learn to reduce my self-preoccupation, pay closer attention to the movements of the Spirit, and grow my ability to love my neighbor as myself.

Caryll Houselander, a twentieth-century Catholic laywoman and mystic, wrote, "Too many anxious Christians today think that their efforts to . . . enter into outward activities can do more to save the world than the surrender of their souls to God, to become Christ-bearers." Maybe it was time to surrender.

I flexed my feet against the curb, and the bird flew off. I stood up and walked inside.

6

Tiny Houses

Simplicity as a Spiritual Discipline

FOR MANY LOW-WAGE EARNERS, TAKING a day off each week—let alone a monthly retreat—is not feasible. Shift workers, including retail staff and service personnel, often work outside of traditional nine-to-five weekday hours, and many low-wage earners work multiple part-time jobs and struggle with high levels of job insecurity. As I spoke to other Christians about Sabbath keeping in contemporary life, many expressed concerns that the practice runs the risk of becoming elitist. A friend who is in seminary told me that she evaluates any spiritual practice according to whether it's accessible to all, including the poor. Using that criterion, a traditional Christian Sabbath observance on Sundays is problematic because it is out of reach for so many people. Only a privileged minority has the ability to take twenty-four hours off on a prescribed day of the week. It is not that my friend wants us to abandon the Sabbath altogether; she has a weekly Sabbath practice herself.

But she wants a more flexible definition of what Sabbath keeping entails. She argues that if we want equity and social justice, we must reimagine how—and importantly, *when*—we invite people into a Sabbath observance. And truthfully, that type of flexibility may benefit all of us. Author and Episcopal priest Barbara Brown Taylor writes, "When I was a parish minister, my only hope of remembering the sabbath was to make it a moveable feast."

Yet the question remains, If we do not observe the Sabbath together on the same day, what do we sacrifice? For one thing, does a "Do what works for you" approach to Sabbath keeping reinforce the idea that it is an individual spiritual practice rather than something intended to be observed in community? More importantly, might we miss out on the radical economic and social implications of Sabbath if we practice it alone?

Walter Brueggemann argues in *Sabbath as Resistance* that a collective Sabbath observance can become a rebellion against the worldly temptations that regularly ensnare us, including the abuses and excesses of industrial capitalism and consumerism. Rather than being elitist, Sabbath is meant to be "the great day of equality when all are equally at rest." In Exodus, the commandment of rest is extended to all—sons and daughters, servants and animals, family and strangers. The implications of this are profound. Fundamentally, Brueggemann writes, the Sabbath is the recognition that "God's people in the world are not commodities to be dispatched for endless production."

In addition to economic justice, rest is central to issues of racial justice as well. Research shows that Black Americans are much more likely to suffer from sleep deprivation than whites. Journalist Maya Kroth argues that we can trace the "racial sleep gap" back to slavery, noting Frederick Douglass's assertion that "more slaves are whipped for oversleeping than any other fault." Tricia Hersey, performance artist, theologian, and founder of the Atlanta-based Nap Ministry, explores the intersection of white supremacy and capitalism. "It wants to use anyone's body as a tool for production," Hersey says. "It wants you to work a hundred hours a week if you can." In this context, Hersey argues that rest is a form of resistance, demonstrating that "our worth [is] not caught up in the grind of capitalism."

On a practical level, author J. Dana Trent notes that if all Christians were to abstain from economic activity during a weekly Sabbath, we could potentially "harness and mimic the enormous economic power of the most successful boycotts." This strategy could help challenge what Trent calls the troubling "merry-go-round" of consumerism itself. My friend Sonia applies this model of economic Sabbath keeping; her rule is that she doesn't shop and declines any invitations to eat at restaurants on Sundays. Her rationale is that all people should have equal opportunity to access the Sabbath, so she doesn't want to use her dollars to encourage stores to stay open.

Of course, there will always be people who have to work on the Sabbath—including clergy and health-care workers. But what if Christians agreed not to *shop* on the Sabbath? How might our economy change? Could this approach become a collective stand against the exploitation of people and natural resources? Could economic Sabbath keeping become an act of solidarity based on the recognition that all of us—and the earth itself—have a God-given right to rest?

Yet some argue that if we abstain from spending money on the Sabbath, we hurt local businesses, which often employ low-wage earners. Returning to a 24/6 economy isn't realistic, and if we advocate for a collective day of economic abstinence, we will inevitably harm others. What about the single parent who has to work on the weekends to even hope to make ends meet? Or the high school student who needs to work to supplement their family's income or save for college? More broadly, some argue, debates about the *when* of Sabbath keeping risk missing the bigger issue of ensuring that people have living wages and affordable housing. As Barbara Ehrenreich wrote in her landmark book *Nickel and Dimed: On (Not) Getting By in America*, "Something is wrong, very wrong, when a . . . person in good health, a person who in addition possesses a working car, can barely support herself by the sweat of her brow. You don't need a degree in economics to see that wages are too low and rents too high."

❖ ❖ ❖

The arguments about Sabbath and economic justice were circling in my head as I departed for my solo retreat that month. I was headed out to Blue Heron Farm, the organic farm and intentional community where I lived for several years after college. My friends Steve and Debbie had a small cabin on the property, where they said I could spend my thirty-six-hour retreat. It was early November, and the day was colder than normal for late autumn in North Carolina. I knew the cabin had electricity and heat, but I packed an extra blanket and my hat and gloves.

I spent the day walking around Blue Heron Farm's sixty-four acres. The land is owned jointly by twelve households. Legally, each family or individual owns the structure in which they live, but the rest of the property is owned and managed in common.

The members follow a cohousing model: they eat group meals each week, make decisions about community resources by consensus, and share space on the property to grow food and raise animals. Most people who live there have jobs off-site that provide income; any money that members earn is theirs to keep.

Even though I loved my time at the farm, I do not idealize community living. After endless consensus-driven meetings that often resulted in interpersonal conflict and community unrest, David and I liked the freedom and privacy we gained when we moved away and bought our own house. David, who is a competent, focused worker and has excellent carpentry skills, often got frustrated by the work style of some of the people at the farm. People often wanted to chat rather than drive forward efficiently during community workdays, and David was frequently dismayed by the quality of the work. We loved the people there, but by the time we left, we were happy we didn't have to live or work with them anymore.

Yet as I walked along the narrow path that traces the creek on the edge of the property, I also reflected on the advantages of living in community. The culture at Blue Heron Farm feels very different from the rest of the world, particularly when it comes to money and material goods. The people in the community seem to want and need a lot less stuff than most of us do, and they are more relaxed about sharing what they do have with others. Washing machines, tractors, garden vegetables, tools, and childcare are all regularly shared. I deeply admire this model and recognize its ecological and interpersonal benefits.

The twelve-foot-by-twelve-foot cabin where I stayed that night had no running water; there was a composting toilet in a detached shed and a small camp stove in an outdoor kitchen. An hour before I went to bed, the electricity in the cabin went out. I trundled over to the main house, and my friend Steve flipped the breaker so that the power was restored. But later, when I was lying in bed, the electricity inexplicably went out again. I didn't feel like getting up and making my way through the dark night again, so I huddled under my blankets and put on my hat. I fell asleep but woke up a few hours later. The cabin had become dramatically colder without the electric heater running, and I was freezing.

I lay awake in the dark. Surprisingly, I didn't feel irritated or stressed. Staring out the small window by my bed at the bright stars, I remembered the days when I lived in a similar cabin as a young woman in my twenties. Although the number of my material possessions, the balance in my bank account, and the physical space where I lived were all much smaller than they are now, I realized my happiness level had been similar. Then and now there were frustrations, stressors, disappointments, and setbacks, just as there were times of joy, peace, and fulfillment. Material wealth did not seem to correlate with contentment. Empirical evidence from around the world suggests something similar: over the long term, people's level of happiness does not substantially increase as material wealth grows.

The experience I had in this community as a young woman radically shaped my mindset. Even as I had worked hard over the past twenty years to succeed in my career and to make a public health impact, I always knew that if I lost my job, I could substantially downsize and still be happy. I could always move back to a smaller space, either literally or figuratively.

Embracing material and spiritual simplicity is both a Christian virtue and a traditional Christian practice. Richard Foster explains that simplicity "is an *inward* reality that results in an *outward* life-style." But like with Sabbath keeping, we've drifted away from embracing simplicity as an intentional spiritual discipline. Lying there in the cold, I wondered how things would change if I prioritized cultivating simplicity in my relationships and spending habits. I would have to give up a lot to streamline my life. While my experience as a young woman at the farm had taught me it was possible, a simplified lifestyle had remained mostly a hypothetical since then. Could I simplify now that I was an adult? Or did family, work, and community responsibilities make this impractical?

I also knew that pursuing simplicity, like engaging in any spiritual practice, can easily become distorted both in intention and in application. Jesus taught that our job is not to be anxious about our lives but rather to "strive first for the kingdom of God and his righteousness" (Matthew 6:33). Foster reminds us of the centrality of this point. He writes that "focus upon [God's] kingdom produces the inward reality, and without the inward reality we will degenerate into legalistic trivia. Nothing else can be central. The desire to get out of the rat race cannot be central, the redistribution of the world's wealth cannot be central, the concern for ecology cannot be central. Seeking *first* God's kingdom and the righteousness, both personal and social, of that kingdom is the only thing that can be central in the spiritual discipline of simplicity."

But what *is* God's kingdom? Foster writes that in order to gain an understanding of the true meaning of the words, we must "destroy the prevailing notion that the Bible is ambiguous about economic issues." Instead, the Bible "challenges nearly every economic value of contemporary society." The exploitation of the poor, the accumulation of wealth, even the absolute right to private property: these are all rejected over and over in Scripture. Throughout his life, Jesus was unequivocal on issues of economic justice. Jesus advises his disciples to "sell your possessions, and give alms. Make purses for yourselves that do not wear out, an unfailing treasure in heaven" (Luke 12:33). Immediately after advising us to love our enemies and turn the other cheek, Jesus tells us to "give to everyone who begs from you" and says if anyone steals from us, we should not seek recompense (Luke 6:30). He consistently admonishes the wealthy and lifts up the impoverished. As Foster writes, "Jesus declared war on the materialism of his day."

One of the most radical manifestations of a vision for economic justice in the Bible is the mandate in the Old Testament for a year of Jubilee, during which debts are forgiven and land is returned to its original owner. God tells Moses that a Jubilee should occur every fifty years, and in the interim, every seventh should be a "Sabbath year" that is a time of rest for the land and the people (Leviticus 25:1–13).

When you read about these concepts, they sound nice, but the possibility of *actually* observing a year of Jubilee or a full year of Sabbath seems both impractical and naive. Yet recent experience suggests otherwise. At the end of the twentieth century, a large-scale international movement called Jubilee 2000 advocated for debt relief for the world's poorest countries. The campaign, which garnered enormous support across more than forty countries, is widely viewed as one of the most effective anti-poverty campaigns of all time. It led to the cancellation of $100 billion of debt for the world's thirty-five poorest countries. The movement—which explicitly drew from Old Testament principles—was supported by a diverse coalition of religious, political, and nonprofit leaders, including Pope John Paul II, Gordon Brown, Bill Clinton, Jeffrey Sachs, Pat Robertson, Bono, and Jesse Helms.

The example is inspirational, and the archbishop of Canterbury, Justin Welby, described the campaign as "perhaps the churches' finest hour in dethroning Mammon," noting that support of Christians of many denominations from around the world was central to the movement. Yet twenty years later, many poor countries are still struggling under crushing debt, and the situation is only getting worse. The work is far from over.

That night in the cabin, I finally fell back asleep despite the cold. In the morning, I stood outside in the small, outdoor kitchen with a blanket around my shoulders while I made a cup of tea. Holding the mug in my hands, I sat in the yard and looked out over the fields. Each blade of grass was tipped with light. Along the horizon, leafless branches fanned against the pink sky.

When I lived on the farm in my early twenties, I was drawn to the lifestyle for the same complicated mix of reasons that I was pursuing a Sabbath year now. I wanted to support economic and ecological justice, but most of all, I wanted a slower pace of life to combat my own chronic stress. But since that time, there had been a major change in my life: I had signed up to be a disciple of Jesus. As such, I knew my Sabbath year had to be about more than just seeking rest and restoration for myself.

Jesus said that we must *first* seek the kingdom of God. I was still learning what that meant, but I wanted to try to figure it out. I wanted to take the next step forward on the journey.

The sun rose, and I stared across the open field. I let the blanket loosen around my shoulders. Sitting in the quiet morning, my mind grew still, and I realized I no longer felt cold.

7

The Promise of Selah

Liberating Rest

IN 2019, THE WORLD HEALTH Organization added "burnout" as an occupational phenomenon for the first time in its International Classification of Diseases. According to their definition, burnout is characterized by "feelings of energy depletion or exhaustion . . . feelings of negativism or cynicism related to one's job, and reduced professional efficacy." The guidelines clarify that this refers "specifically to phenomena in the occupational context."

This recognition from the leading international health authority is both important and painfully ironic. In my own career in global public health, I often wonder if—in both overt and subtle ways—we are promoting workaholism around the world.

I wonder this when a colleague who leads a large maternal and child health project in East Africa tells me he has to work through the Christmas holiday to respond to changes his donor requested in their program design. Or when another colleague who manages an HIV care and treatment program in Zambia emails me on a Saturday morning with an apology and explanation that she is so overextended, she didn't have time to respond to my question earlier in the week. Over the last decade, I have observed the pace of communication speed up as colleagues around the world exchange information in real time via WhatsApp, Skype, Twitter, GoToMeeting, LinkedIn, Zoom, and Microsoft Teams. During group conference calls, I regularly have more than one private sidebar chat going on to exchange observations and information with colleagues. After receiving an email from a colleague, I frequently receive an instant message from the same person a few minutes later with more information to provide context or to ask when I think I'll be able to respond to their query. The world is getting smaller and faster, and the expectation is we all need to keep up.

Aside from the spiritual dimensions of rest, public health professionals—theoretically—recognize the importance of downtime. Evidence clearly shows that chronic sleep deprivation can dramatically increase our risk of heart disease, obesity, dementia, and mental illness. Likewise, research indicates that workplace burnout can contribute to a myriad of illnesses and problems, including diabetes, musculoskeletal pain, heart disease, chronic headaches, respiratory problems, insomnia, depression, and absenteeism. We are not machines, and we must rest to function well.

Yet there are huge and pressing challenges to address in our work, so how much time can we afford to take away to rest? We have limited resources, and our lives are short. Most of us working in public health and global development sincerely want to use the limited time we have to help solve the biggest social problems that plague humanity: poverty, health and educational inequities, environmental degradation, gender-based violence, humanitarian crises. And we want to achieve greater efficiency and sophistication in our problem-solving efforts in order to achieve substantial, large-scale impact. But what is the human cost of the breakneck speeds we maintain in order to do so?

Does it become a question of trade-offs? Should the goal be to maximize our efficiency even in how and when we rest so that we can quickly recharge our batteries and get back to work? Is an expansive Sabbath lifestyle one we can really afford to embrace if we want to solve our most pressing global problems?

◆ ◆ ◆

I met Hassana the day after I arrived in Abuja, Nigeria. A beautiful woman and an accomplished professional, she was wearing a striking light blue African dress and matching head wrap embroidered with silver and gold. She exuded both kindness and authority as we chatted over a cup of tea. She had just announced to the local staff that she would be leaving her role as director of the country office of our organization to take a senior leadership position in the Nigerian government. We met to discuss my project activities, and we chatted about her upcoming transition.

A colleague in the meeting with us mentioned that in her new job, Hassana would essentially be responsible for the well-being of two hundred million Nigerians. I gulped and sat back in my chair, contemplating his words. Hassana seemed relaxed, and she smiled warmly as we shook hands goodbye. I searched her face for stress or anxiety, wondering how she would balance it all. If I had anywhere near the level of responsibility she was assuming, I would not be as calm.

Predictions indicate that by 2050, the population of Nigeria, currently the seventh most populous country in the world, will grow to three hundred million, replacing the United States as the third-largest country in the world. Despite some recent economic growth, the challenges facing Nigeria are daunting. Rampant poverty and income inequality, inadequate infrastructure, and social and political unrest stymie the country's progress. In 2019, the World Bank gave Nigeria a ranking of 152 out of 157 on its Human Capital Index, which measures indicators such as investments in education and health care. Nigeria has the second-largest HIV epidemic in the world and is the second-largest contributor to the under-five and maternal mortality rates globally. The Boko Haram insurgency in the Northeast has led to a terrible humanitarian crisis, with over 3.3 million people displaced and with violence continuing to terrorize local populations.

During my stay in Nigeria, thirty people were killed in a roadside attack in Borno State. CNN reported that among those killed was Fatima Babagana, a nineteen-year-old university student who was studying political science and wanted to become a journalist. When I read the article, I couldn't stop staring at the image of Fatima. In the photograph, she is wearing a stylish dress and headscarf and holding her iPhone and a leather purse. She was traveling with her uncle when she was killed; they were stopped at a military checkpoint because they had missed the four o'clock curfew and were not allowed to continue driving on to the next village. They parked the car and planned to spend the night. They were attacked several hours later. Fatima's uncle told the reporter that "Fatima was sitting in the backseat and typing on her phone. They saw the light from the phone because it was very dark. Next thing I knew, they had shot her in the head."

While I was in Nigeria, I remained in Abuja, the capital city, which is in the central part of the country and several hours from the area where Boko Haram is most active. Yet crime and violence remain an issue even in the capital. Before I left, our security team told me that the most common threat is kidnapping for ransom. Both Nigerians and foreigners are frequently targeted. Because of the risks, I decided to spend my Sabbath retreat that month sequestered in the hotel.

◆ ◆ ◆

Typically, when I travel for work and have a weekend off, I use the time for sightseeing. But in Abuja, I decided not to venture out. I felt an obligation to my worried family back home to be cautious. And since I hadn't yet taken a Sabbath retreat that month, I decided to embrace the downtime. It was an odd sensation. Partly, I felt claustrophobic and embarrassed about my self-imposed house arrest, but mostly, I was painfully aware of my immense privilege. Right outside the hotel, there were armed guards who maintained a "secure perimeter" for the hotel. Meanwhile, I ate spaghetti and drank beer by the pool.

The protection my wealth and nationality afforded me that weekend wasn't the only privilege I spent time reflecting on. The same weekend I was in Nigeria, a group from my church back in Chapel Hill, North Carolina, was making a pilgrimage to Montgomery, Alabama, to visit the National Memorial for Peace and Justice. The lynching memorial there, which opened to the public in 2018, commemorates the more than four thousand Black people who were murdered by white mobs starting in the late 1800s through the mid-1900s. I was more than five thousand miles away, but my heart and mind were with my friends who were on their way to Montgomery by bus. Between us was the Atlantic Ocean, where the transatlantic slave trade transported an estimated twelve million Africans to the Americas between the sixteenth and nineteenth centuries. The legacy of the slave trade on the demographic, economic, political, and social structures of Africa was devastating; it had made many countries, including Nigeria, vulnerable to later European colonization, and it continues to shape the trajectory of the region. As the Kenyan writer Ngũgĩ wa Thiong'o notes, "It is not a strange coincidence that the victims of the slave trade and slavery on the African continent and abroad are collectively the ones experiencing underdevelopment."

As the descendant of slaveholders, I am the direct beneficiary of generations of wealth that resulted from my ancestors inflicting unspeakable violence on other humans, stealing their labor, tearing their families apart, and denying them their most basic rights and dignities. As Mary Elliott and Jazmine Hughes wrote in the *New York Times*'s 1619 Project, "From one century to the next, [families] profited from enslaved people, their wealth passing from generation to generation. As enslaved families were torn apart, white people . . . were building capital, a legacy that continues today."

The legacy of race- and class-based privilege is part of what allowed me to be in Abuja that weekend. During the Jim Crow era, while African Americans were routinely denied opportunities for economic advancement and terrorized by lynchings across the country, my great-grandfather was making a career for himself at Esso, the precursor to ExxonMobil. In 1955, one of ExxonMobil's subsidiaries began commercial operations in Nigeria; today, the company is one of the country's largest oil producers. The stock options my great-grandfather earned were passed down to my grandfather and father, and they helped pay for my college tuition.

As such, I embody much of the complexity and hypocrisy of "global development" work, given that my own family's complicity in white supremacy and white privilege is, in part, what allowed me to be in sub-Saharan Africa on that trip. At its core, my work in Nigeria was an attempt to help reverse the impact of centuries of violence and injustice. Given this, what did it mean to take my Sabbath retreat sequestered in an expensive hotel behind walls lined with barbed wire and with armed men standing guard? Was resting in this way and in this context an act of profound hypocrisy and self-indulgence? Even if I was trying to make a positive difference through my public health work, I was undeniably a part of a system that was built on the worst abuses of humans and continues to be fueled by the exploitation of people and our planet.

A friend of mine at church once told me that she thinks of sin as a virus. There is no cell in our bodies that is not infected. Given this, is there any way to escape it? Was my time of rest in Abuja doing anything to increase shalom in my heart or in the world?

◆ ◆ ◆

While I was in Nigeria, I watched the video of a sermon that Rev. Howard John Wesley, the pastor of the historic Alfred Street Baptist Church in Alexandria, Virginia, gave on the topic of selah. Pastor Wesley explained that the word *selah* shows up in Scripture seventy-four times, almost all of them in the book of Psalms. There is no definitive translation of *selah*, but because the Psalms were meant to be sung, selah essentially served as a musical notation to indicate that it was time to pause and take a breath. "Selah is a call to rest," Rev. Wesley explains in his sermon, and we shouldn't be surprised with the repetitive use of the word because throughout the Bible, "God is always calling God's people to rest." Wesley reminds us that in Exodus, one of the first things God did after freeing the people of Israel from slavery was tell them to rest. Why? Because, he explains, "they had been slaves, and the one thing that slaves do not get to do is rest." God told the people that they needed to learn to rest because "whatever you can't rest from, you're a slave to." To be God's people is to be free, and we can't be free without rest.

Wesley's message reminded me of what Tricia Hersey says about the revolutionary power of rest. She says embracing rest is critical because it "disrupts and pushes back and allows space for healing, for invention, for us to be more human. It allows us to imagine this new world that we want, this new world that's liberated, that's full of justice."

Rest also allows us to regain an ability to listen to our bodies. In an interview with the *Atlantic*, Hersey argues that "white supremacy and capitalism have stolen not only our rest, but also our intuition. . . . Part of this rest resistance is . . . knowing there's always time for you to reclaim your body as yours."

While I was sitting sequestered in my hotel in Nigeria, I exchanged WhatsApp messages with my friend Liz back in the United States. Liz was the victim of a violent crime in her twenties. As part of her own healing process, as well as her commitment to broader community healing, she now spends part of her time on restorative justice projects. She has formed a life-changing friendship with a man who was convicted of a violent crime and was sentenced to thirty-seven years in prison. Liz and the man have shared their stories with one another; they exchange regular letters, and she visits him in prison when she can. During our text exchange, Liz told me she's not sure where the friendship will take them, but she knows that they are on a journey and that they are "going together."

Her words stuck with me. *Going together.* As I sat in my hotel room, I reflected on the week of work I had just completed. I thought about all the people I had met and collaborated with in meetings, planning sessions, and clinic site visits. Hassana. Mariya. Anthony. Jennifer. Helen. Kumeh. They had each impressed me with their passion, intelligence, drive, competence, and commitment. As a colleague who had grown up in Lagos, the largest city in Nigeria, had said to me with a smile, "You have to love the Nigerian hustle." Yes, that was it. I loved the hustle I had felt among everyone I had encountered that week. It felt like the same type of hustle I often observe in myself. The previous Wednesday evening, I had stayed up until nearly midnight preparing for our meeting the next day, and several of my coworkers did the same. And the hard work had paid off; we had moved a collective agenda forward, and it looked like the government would sign off on the plan we had developed together.

I am not sure if or how humans will ever fully recover from the virus of sin that infects each of us and our world. When I pray about this, I see an image of us moving through the jagged edges of all that is violent and fragmented in the world and in us straight to a place beyond all that, which I imagine is the heart of God. In our day-to-day work, I feel God's presence as I glimpse signs that we are getting better at going together. This gives me hope.

So that weekend in Abuja, despite all the unfinished work and despite the pervasive sinfulness I recognize in myself and in the world, I allowed myself to rest. I still had so many questions and concerns, including about my own complicity in systems of injustice and what to do about it. But I also remembered Rev. Wesley's words: whatever we can't rest from, we are slaves to. God is always calling God's people to liberation and to rest. We have to heed the call.

8

A Double Mitzvah

Sex and the Sabbath

THE MOST CONSISTENT PART OF my Sabbath retreats was the level of exhaustion I felt as I began them. I continued to careen through life at a relentless pace, and while I loved the experience of taking time away each month, I wasn't sure the approach was making a sustained difference. The retreats were restorative in the short term, but their effects didn't usually last long. Daily life remained incredibly busy and demanding, and I wasn't sure how to make the peace I experienced during the selah pauses "stick." If I kept at it, I wondered, would the practice transform me at a more fundamental level over time? Or was a bigger, structural change in my life required?

In the meantime, I often did not have time to plan my monthly retreats until a few days or, in one case, a few hours beforehand. One month the schedule was so packed that I wasn't able to reserve thirty-six hours to get away. Looking at the calendar, I realized I only had one free afternoon open that month, and it was later that day.

So at the last minute, I called my friend Abigail and asked if I could come take a nap in her guest room. I didn't provide an explanation, and surprisingly, she didn't ask any questions. When I arrived, she showed me in and left me alone. I lay down on the four-poster bed and slept for two and a half hours. When I woke up, the afternoon sun was bright on the sheets. I read a few pages of the book I had brought with me: my favorite devotional by Caryll Houselander. My eyes rested on these words: "Pray for us, holy Mother of God." I left the book open on my chest and stared at the light streaming through the vaulted window until it was time to go home.

The other consistent aspect of my Sabbath retreats, whether abbreviated or full length, was solitude. For the first seven months of the experiment, I always went away by myself. I spent one retreat in a tiny, historic church near my house; the congregation allowed anyone to use their space for silent prayer during the week. No one else was there the day I went, and I lay on the floor in the back of the sanctuary, staring out of the simple stained glass window. I spent another weekend in Paris on my way back to the United States from a work trip in Senegal. I had been scheduled to stay an extra week in West Africa, but the hotel where colleagues and I were staying had received a credible terrorist threat, and the conference I was going to attend had been canceled. When the airline rebooked my ticket, I impetuously added a one-night layover in Paris. I got in late at night and spent the next day walking the streets of the city, following paths along the Seine. The tiny hotel room I had booked was several blocks from the Eiffel Tower, so I wandered around the city without a map or an agenda without being worried about getting lost. When I was ready to return, I simply looked up across the cityscape, saw the tower, and headed that way.

Over the months, taking these retreats had made me realize how starved I was for alone time. My life was full of people: at home, at work, at church, in the broader community. People who lived locally, and people who lived far away. People I connected to via phone calls, coffee dates, text messages, work meetings, Facebook, church meetings, conferences, Twitter, and spontaneous interactions at the grocery store. My days were jammed with human connection of all kinds, and they included many different dynamics. On any given day, interactions could be stressful, loving, inspiring, draining, time-consuming, soulful, disappointing, worrisome, humorous, aggravating, or shocking. And when I woke up in the morning, I usually could not predict what emotional tenor the day would have. The volume and speed of my email correspondence meant that at any moment, without notice, I could be plunged into anxiety by some unexpected deadline or thrilled by some exciting bit of news.

Likewise, family life could be turbulent, swinging from relaxed companionship in one moment to flared tension and misunderstanding the next. As in other areas of my life, I couldn't reliably predict when the dynamics would shift. My husband and I would be teasing each other good-naturedly, and the next minute, one of us would be hurt. Every day was an adventure, and often it was an exhausting one.

It didn't help that when I was overwhelmed at work, I would often become irritable with David. I viewed him as one of the few "safe" people in my life, the one to whom I could expose and express my built-up stress. David tried to be patient and understanding, but the cumulative impact was wearing on him, and our busy schedules meant we had limited time and energy for each other. We tried to create intentional time for our marriage, but David often complained that it wasn't enough. He missed me, and he wanted me to prioritize our time together. He wanted more time for physical intimacy. His requests were reasonable, and I was grateful to have such a loving partner, but I was so tired. I found myself craving more solitude rather than more intimacy. As a result, our needs often did not align. David continued to express his desire and disappointment, and I felt increasingly guilty and pressured. There was no easy solution, and we found ourselves stuck in a painful, circular dynamic.

As I contemplated if and how my Sabbath retreats could have a more lasting impact on my life, I wondered if I also needed to take a retreat *with* David. He had been gracious about my yearlong experiment and generous in taking care of the kids and household while I was away, but over the long term, I realized the structure would likely not be sustainable for our family. I needed to find ways to make more time for myself *and* to make more time for my marriage. Both were precious to me, and I didn't want to neglect either. So one month David and I planned a Sabbath retreat together.

◆ ◆ ◆

If you only believed what you read in the newspapers, you'd think that Christians are obsessed with sex—in particular, who should and shouldn't have sex with whom and when. Yet my lived experience as a recently baptized Christian is that human sexuality rarely, if ever, comes up at church. Maybe evangelicals talk about sex a lot, but mainline Protestants don't seem to.

As a public health professional who works to promote sexual health and expand access to contraception, I'm surprised that sexuality is not discussed from the pulpit, in Bible study, in adult education classes, or, as far as I can tell, during religious education for the children and youth. We talk about a lot of other things related to our spiritual and emotional well-being, including love of neighbor and formation in Christ, but we don't talk about how sexuality fits into all of this. Maybe those conversations are happening without me, but I doubt it. Over the past eight years, I have gone to almost every adult forum session, and I have scoured all the titles in our church library. It seems like my church, at least, is pretty silent on the topic.

Maybe I missed the bulk of the discussion about sex, at least within my denomination. I was baptized in 2012, nine years after the diocese of New Hampshire elected the first openly gay bishop, Rev. Gene Robinson. The decision sparked enormous controversy, but the denomination pressed on in expanding rights for LGBTQ people. In 2009, a formal statement affirming same-sex couples was adopted at the Episcopal General Convention, and in 2012, a liturgy for blessing the relationships of same-sex couples was adopted. This journey wasn't easy; from what I've heard, the debate exhausted and divided my own congregation and congregations around the country, ultimately leading to a formal schism within the Anglican Communion. Now a similar dynamic is unfolding within the United Methodist Church. In early 2020, the church announced that the denomination would split over "fundamental differences" regarding gay marriage and the role of LGBTQ clergy.

I am incredibly thankful to everyone who has and who continues to advocate tirelessly to expand LGBTQ rights in the church and in the broader world. It seems like a no-brainer that individuals of any sexual orientation or gender expression deserve all the recognition, love, respect, and standing in the church that any straight or cisgender person receives. At the same time, issues around sexual orientation—including gay marriage and ordination of LGBTQ clergy—seem to me like only a small component of a broader discussion that needs to happen within the church about love, relationships, and sexuality. As a new Christian, I wanted to know, What does the church have to say about what healthy, loving, respectful, safe, fun, Christ-filled sexuality should look and feel like?

Of course, countless Christians and former Christians have been deeply wounded by the responses the church has given to questions about sexuality. Several of my friends identify themselves as being "in recovery" because they grew up in the purity culture embraced and promoted in many evangelical churches today. Author Amy Peterson writes in her book *Where Goodness Still Grows* that during her own evangelical upbringing, "if a pastor or youth pastor preached about staying pure, you could be sure he was not speaking broadly about holiness." Rather, purity had a "singular meaning": virginity until marriage. The upshot was that sex was often presented as spiritually dangerous and potentially dirty. Peterson writes, "Purity culture intends—at its best—to keep adolescent mistakes from hampering the health of a marriage. But, instead, it often sends kids . . . into adulthood burdened with other baggage: shame, anxiety, pressure, and even terror." She goes on to explain that some people "take years to recover from the damaging messages they internalized about sex. Some have sought escape through self-harm and even suicide." More broadly, Peterson writes that the use of the word *purity* can be problematic when it comes to messages about sex. She explains that in general, human reactions are

> conditioned by what researchers call dose insensitivity and negativity dominance. Dose insensitivity is the idea that it only takes a single drop of a containment to effectively ruin something. . . . If a drop of urine is added to a liter of soda, most people will not drink that soda. A single drop of something unclean is more powerful than a much larger quantity of something clean. For teenagers, this response might translate into a belief that the smallest sexual purity infraction can make them utterly gross and beyond fixing. Once that drop of urine is in the Coke, it's ruined beyond repair.

Christians who grew up in a purity culture can end up feeling like they are similarly contaminated.

My own upbringing in the Unitarian Universalist Church was radically different from this. When I was thirteen years old, I participated in the standard religious education program offered to eighth graders, which included a semester-long course called About Your Sexuality. The curriculum was comprehensive and evidence based. We talked about everything: masturbation, birth control, monogamy, sex before marriage, gender identity, same-sex relationships, and communication skills. It was great. As a result, I launched into adolescence and young adulthood believing that sex was natural, beautiful, and sacred. I viewed sex as something that was typically wonderful as long as it took place in the context of a loving relationship in which both partners were committed to keeping themselves and the other person safe, both physically and emotionally.

The perspective I gained as a young person served me well throughout my life. Now David and I have been married for over sixteen years and together as a couple for twenty. Despite several major challenges we had faced in our relationship as well as the daily stressors we continue to navigate, I feel very happily married. As part of this, David and I generally have a fun, loving, and enjoyable sex life.

Yet despite this, navigating the question of *when* to have sex can be stressful and painful for both of us. The *when* of sex is easy for David. His answer is anytime. My answer is more complicated and nuanced, and over the years, I've come to recognize a pattern. Typically, I do not want to have sex when I'm tired or stressed out. And I'm tired and stressed a lot of the time, so that makes things tough. Apparently, I'm not alone. A recent cover article in the *Atlantic*, "The Sex Recession," suggests that Americans of all ages are having sex less frequently than they did in the past. This trend has been observed across all age groups—from teens to baby boomers. The author of the article, Kate Julian, writes that since the late 1990s, "the average adult went from having sex 62 times a year to 54 times. A given person may not notice this decrease, but nationally it adds up to a lot of missing sex." In talking with experts around the country as part of her research for the article, Julian heard many theories about the reasons for this trend. She wrote, "I was told it might be a consequence of the hookup culture, of crushing economic pressures, of surging anxiety rates, of psychological frailty, of widespread antidepressant use, of streaming television, of environmental estrogens leaked by plastics, of dropping testosterone levels, of digital porn, of the vibrator's golden age, of dating apps, of option paralysis, of helicopter parents, of careerism, of smartphones, of the news cycle, of information overload generally, of sleep deprivation, of obesity."

This list is fairly exhaustive, but I wondered if the author was missing an important culprit. Could the sex recession be linked to a decreasing emphasis on rest, including Sabbath keeping? What if there is a relatively simple solution to much of what ails us as a culture in terms of sex. What if we made more time for sex when we're wide awake and well rested?

In Jewish culture, sex on the Sabbath is considered a "double mitzvah," which means that not only is it viewed as a blessing; it is actively recommended by rabbinical tradition as an important, sacred activity to engage in on the Sabbath. Similarly, I wondered if the church could get behind celebrating sex as part of a sacred Sabbath observance. In my own life, making time for sex on the Sabbath turned out to be a game changer.

◆ ◆ ◆

The month that David and I planned our Sabbath retreat together, we were in New England visiting my parents. My stepson, Soren, was back at home in North Carolina with his mom, and my parents had offered to watch our daughter, Lila, so we could get away for a night. We gratefully accepted.

I had rented a place on Airbnb in a little town about an hour away, and we drove there on a cold, rainy Saturday morning. The traffic was heavy, and David and I were both tense as we navigated the unfamiliar route. We arrived just after lunch and carried our bags up the uneven staircase on the outside of the building. The space we had rented was a single loft room in an old, renovated barn. Looking around, I immediately fell in love with the place. At one end of the room was a small kitchen

with dark marble counters, stylish white cabinets, and a gleam-
ing gas stove. There was an antique farm table in the corner
with a bouquet of irises in the center. The table was already set
for two. I looked out the small window above the kitchen sink.
There was a stream running along the edge of the property and
a field of wildflowers just beyond.

At the other end of the room were a queen-size bed and a
small sitting area with a couch and two chairs. The ceiling of
the loft was tall, with four skylights providing natural light.
There was a small shelf of books, and among them was a novel
I had always wanted to read and one of my favorite collections
of poetry. The proprietor had left us tea, coffee, and a bottle of
wine on the counter. We had bought fresh bread, cheese, olives,
and cookies at the market on our way into town. David fixed us
some tea as I took off my shoes and socks. I looked around, a
sense of delight growing in me. The place was perfect. Heaven.
The room looked like it belonged in a magazine, and it was
ours for almost two full days. We were alone, and we had no
plans. I lay down in the bed, taking it all in.

David put my cup of tea on the bedside table. He took off
his own shoes and socks and settled on the couch to read the
notebook with the instructions the owners had left. I looked
over at him. He seemed relaxed, and I could feel my shoulders
loosen. We were not in a rush to go anywhere or do anything.
Whenever David and I scheduled an extended period of time
to hang out, we always did well together. We enjoyed each
other's company and rarely had conflict. It was only when
we tried to squeeze in quality time late at night or between
errands and activities on the weekend that we had a difficult time connecting. Now there wasn't any pressure or rush,
and I felt the difference it made. David picked up a book off

the shelf and read the back cover. Fifteen minutes later, I was asleep.

❖ ❖ ❖

When I read Bromleigh McCleneghan's book *Good Christian Sex*, I finally found a straightforward explanation of a theology of sexuality that made sense to me. McCleneghan, a church pastor and author, points out that early Christian theologians were deeply influenced by the Greek philosophers that pre-dated them. She explains that a number of "Greek schools of thought believed that existence was divided into matter and antimatter—material things and spiritual things. The spiritual things, the ideas, Truth and Beauty, those things were unchanging, pure, lovely and good. Bodies—which women seemed to have a harder time transcending by virtue of childbearing—were 'profane,' ever changing, subjective." Yet McCleneghan goes on to say, "As much as those early Christians were influenced by body/soul dualism," the "far more enduring theological conviction is that our souls, minds and hearts are intertwined." This is the heart of Christian incarnational theology, she says— namely, that Jesus was both fully human and fully divine. One implication of the incarnation is "God creates us in the divine image, creates us with bodies, creates us through earth and divine breath, creates us good."

Yes. The explanation seemed so simple, and yet it made so much sense. Jesus was God incarnated in human form, so *of course* bodies are good. And because our bodies are a gift from God, our sexuality is a gift as well. Enough said. Right?

The problem, author A. J. Swoboda points out, is that people "fall into the same trap time and again—not knowing how to enjoy a gift from God." Swoboda says the same is true with the gift of Sabbath rest. In his book *Subversive Sabbath*, he writes, "The Sabbath is a gift we do not know how to receive. In a world of doing, going and producing, we have no use for a gift that invites us to stop."

When I took the retreat with David during my Sabbath year, I was reminded of these two gifts we receive from God: the gift of rest and the gift of our bodies. I am usually so busy doing, going, and producing that I don't give David and our marriage the best parts of myself. Instead, I give him the tired, irritable, leftover parts. That needed to change.

Having a thirty-six-hour retreat together in the loft far away from home was wonderful, but it was not real life. Time together during a weekly Sabbath, I realized, could be key. So after we got home from the trip, I committed to making time for our marriage during each weekly Sabbath. In general, I realized, time spent together in the afternoons was best for me. When I first wake up in the mornings, I feel frumpy and eager for coffee; this is not my best time for intimacy. By the evening, I'm often too tired to have meaningful connection. In contrast, during the afternoons, I am awake, have energy, and am more emotionally and physically available.

I recently asked my friend Josh, who grew up in a Jewish home, what he did as a kid during the Sabbath. He said that on Saturday afternoons, after going to synagogue in the mornings, he loved playing long, complicated board games with his cousins. I asked what his parents did during that time. He said that they would read or would take a nap. I asked him if he thought "taking a nap" might ever have been code for sex. Josh shook his head adamantly. He couldn't (or didn't want to) picture his parents engaging in a double mitzvah on those Sabbath afternoons.

But I wasn't so sure Josh was right. A few weeks later, I asked my friend Rachel about her family's Sabbath observance. Rachel has three adult children, and while her kids were growing up, her family had a regular Sabbath observance.

"Did you ever use naptime as an excuse for sex on the Sabbath?" I asked.

She grinned widely, saying, "Most definitely. 'Naps' on the Sabbath were the best."

So what do David and I tell our kids when we sneak away during Sabbath afternoons? I've found that most kids—whether they are young or teenagers—understand and respect the power of naps. David and I tell the kids that we're tired, and they've never thought to question it. I just hope they don't read this book—at least until they are older. I don't want the cover for our Sabbath mitzvah to be blown.

9

Viewing the Totality

A Glimpse of a Quieter Life

THE FOLLOWING MONTH WAS THE last Sabbath retreat in my scheduled yearlong experiment, and I decided I wanted to spend it with my family. That month, people around the country were buzzing with excitement because a total solar eclipse—during which the moon would completely cover the disk of the sun—was scheduled to take place. A total eclipse had not been visible from the mainland United States since 1979. Plus, this eclipse would be visible in a band that spanned the entire contiguous United States, from the Pacific to the Atlantic coasts. That had not happened for nearly a century.

David and the kids wanted to drive the five hours from our house to a location in South Carolina where we would be able to see the eclipse. I was ambivalent about making the trip, not sure if it was worth the time or effort. But they were insistent, and I decided to follow their lead.

When we arrived in the tiny town just over the state line, it was midafternoon. Rather than proceeding on to a bigger city in South Carolina, we had decided to go to the closest place on the map where we would be in the "zone of totality." There were no restaurants or stores in the town, just a small gas station where we stopped to use the bathroom and buy sodas and chips. When we had googled the location, we read that the population was 206.

We proceeded to a nearby park and pulled into the shade under the only tree on the small street. The air was hot and dry. We had arrived early and had several hours to wait. Lila got out and sat on the hood of the car, scanning the landscape. There wasn't much to see: just a small picnic pavilion and a single swing set.

In her classic 1979 essay "Total Eclipse," Annie Dillard wrote about her experience viewing a full eclipse in Washington State that year. She explained that several years before, she had seen a partial eclipse, and there was no comparison between the two. She wrote, "Seeing a partial eclipse bears the same relation to seeing a total eclipse as kissing a man does to marrying him, or as flying in an airplane does to falling out of an airplane. Although the one experience precedes the other, it in no way prepares you for it."

Later, after we saw the totality, I agreed with Dillard. Yet for me, the sweetest part of that day in South Carolina was the people we encountered. After we sat listlessly in the park pavilion for over an hour, eating our gas station snacks, people started arriving. First a married couple from upstate New York. They were both science teachers and had driven eighteen hours to see the totality. Then a mother and daughter who lived nearby. They brought their homemade eclipse-viewing devices, which they had constructed out of cereal boxes. Then the mayor of the town showed up. She was a lively, middle-aged African American woman who greeted us warmly. She explained that she had grown up in the town but had moved away and lived up north for many years. Now she was back and enjoyed serving her community in a leadership position. Her energy and enthusiasm made the pavilion suddenly feel festive. We had come together as strangers and were about to witness a cosmic event together. The ninety-eight-degree afternoon still felt oppressively hot, but now I began to feel a spark as the anticipation grew.

We still had nearly two hours to wait, though, and as we sat there, I thought about the audiobook we had listened to together on the drive down to South Carolina: Susan Cain's best-selling book *Quiet: The Power of Introverts in a World That Can't Stop Talking*. I had been eager to share the book with Lila for many years but had waited until I hoped she was old enough to understand and appreciate it. Lila is a textbook introvert. She is temperamentally quiet. She is thoughtful, doesn't rush in to insert her opinion or personality in social situations, and can easily become exhausted by group interactions. She loves to read, make artwork, and listen to podcasts on a variety of topics. She is eager to talk with David and me about big, philosophical questions. She is wise, insightful, and funny, but strangers can easily miss these qualities because she is typically reserved around new people, particularly in crowds. She has always been this way, and ever since she was in preschool, I worried that teachers and peers might label her as "shy." The truth is, Lila is not shy in that she's not typically anxious in social settings. She's just quiet.

But we live in a culture that venerates extroversion. In *Quiet*, Cain argues that we need to challenge this and change the broader narrative about introversion. In describing different personality traits, Cain explains that introverts often "have strong social skills and enjoy parties and business meetings, but after a while wish they were home in their pajamas. They prefer to devote their social energies to close friends, colleagues, and family. They listen more than they talk, think before they speak." Cain also describes people who are "highly sensitive," most of whom are introverts. She writes that "the highly sensitive tend to be philosophical or spiritual in their orientation, rather than materialistic or hedonistic. They dislike small talk. They often describe themselves as creative or intuitive. . . . They love music, nature, art, physical beauty. They feel exceptionally strong emotions—sometimes acute bouts of joy, but also sorrow, melancholy, and fear. Highly sensitive people also process information about their environments—both physical and emotional—unusually deeply. They tend to notice subtleties that others miss—another person's shift in mood, say, or a lightbulb burning a touch too brightly." These qualities can all be tremendous strengths, but in our schools and workplaces, we often devalue them. Introversion is frequently viewed as "a second-class personality trait, somewhere between a disappointment and a pathology." This is a huge mistake, Cain argues, because over and over throughout history, introverts have made many of the best and most influential contributions to society. Cain makes a data-driven argument that there is "zero correlation between the gift of gab and good ideas."

I wanted Lila to internalize these messages. I hoped the book would help her feel confident and proud of who she is. I also wanted to listen to the book for more self-focused reasons. I had read it before but needed to hear its message again. For most of my life, I've identified as an extrovert. I like to talk, and

I often get energy from social interactions. I know my extroverted qualities can sometimes be problematic; I like being the center of attention, and I can take up more than my share of space and airtime. I try to be mindful about not interrupting people, but I frequently rush in too quickly to express my opinion or interject to respond to someone else's point. I often think out loud—which is helpful for me, but I am sure can be tedious for others. And there is an energetic cost. Increasingly, over time, I found that my extroverted lifestyle can leave me feeling enervated. In many ways, this is not surprising. As author Elizabeth Gilbert writes, "Silence and solitude are universally recognized spiritual practices, and there are good reasons for this. Learning how to discipline your speech is a way of preventing your energy from spilling out of you through the rupture of your mouth, exhausting you and filling the world with words, words, words instead of serenity [and] peace."

Beyond these problems, I recognized my tendency to overextend myself socially. I love being with people, but I reach a threshold where I have no more energy to give to others. And I'm not good at recognizing when I've gone too far or when I'm getting close to my limit. David often becomes impatient when he finds me talking on the phone or texting or planning a social gathering soon after listening to me complain that I'm exhausted. He doesn't understand why I can't do a better job at self-regulation, and he constantly urges me to scale back.

After my yearlong experiment of taking Sabbath retreats, I had started to notice a shift in myself. Remarkably, I felt quieter. I was starting to socialize less and to seek more time for quiet as part of my weekly routine. I wasn't sure what these changes might mean over the long term, but I wanted to lean into this new experience. I wanted to cultivate the nascent sense of stillness.

That day in South Carolina, as the moon began to cover the sun, we all moved out from under the pavilion to the center of the field. The light grew dim, and the air cooled dramatically. The colors around us became strange. We knew the only safe time to take off our protective eye gear during the eclipse was during the totality, when the sun was completely blocked by the moon. As that occurred, we slowly removed our special glasses. We all laughed in astonishment as we looked around at one another. We were standing in the middle of a cold, dark field that just moments before had been hot and bright. Strange shadows moved like water through the grass. The color and quality of the light was something I had never seen before. The moment was over quickly, but for a few minutes, we saw a different world.

The experience was similar to what my Sabbath year had given me: a new view of a familiar landscape. A glimpse of a different way of life. A life with more quiet and stillness and more space and time for God.

When the novelist Flannery O'Connor was a young woman, she kept a spiritual journal. In it, she wrote a series of prayers including this reflection: "Dear God, I cannot love Thee the way I want to. You are the slim crescent of a moon that I see and my self is the earth's shadow that keeps me from seeing all the moon. The crescent is very beautiful . . . but what I am afraid of, dear God, is that my self shadow will grow so large that it blocks the whole moon. . . . I do not know you God because I am in the way. Please help me to push myself aside."

Like O'Connor, I don't want my shadow self to create an eclipse that blocks out God's light. The challenge for all of us is to allow our sense of self, which we usually grip so tightly, to be pushed aside. This is what Sabbath helps accomplish. Sabbath rest creates a shift in our lives so that we no longer see our-selves as the center of the universe. Instead, we experience a new alignment of the heavenly bodies and, in the process, dis-cover a transformed landscape on the earth below.

As I ended my yearlong experiment of intentional Sabbath retreats, I didn't want to lose this insight or the growing sense of quiet I had gained. I didn't want to forget what a powerful eclipse rest provides. Instead, I wanted to learn how to integrate Sabbath keeping more fully into everyday life. Because as it turned out, a crisis was looming that would upend everything.

Part III

EVERYDAY SABBATH

10

Beyond Mommy Guilt

A Cure for Compulsivity?

URING THE MONTH WHEN COVID-19 hit the United States in full force, I was scheduled to take Lila on a weekend camping trip. Around the world, people were starting to recognize the severity of the pandemic, and big changes were implemented almost overnight. School districts around the country announced lengthy closures. Everyone in my office was mandated to work from home. But the governor in our state hadn't yet told us all to shelter in place; that wouldn't happen until the following week. In the meantime, state campgrounds were still open. So I decided to proceed with our camping trip. It was early spring, and based on past experience, I knew the location where we had a reservation wouldn't be crowded. Plus, camping seemed like an ideal way to practice social distancing, and we were already stir-crazy from being inside all week. I invited David and Soren to join us, but they wanted to stay home to work on a project in the backyard, so Lila and I headed out by ourselves.

When we arrived at the campground, we lay on a blanket on the grass while Lila read *Calvin and Hobbes* and ate Ritz Crackers. I looked up at the sky and thought about everything that had been happening. Before we left, Lila and I had stopped at the grocery store to buy provisions. As we walked from the parking lot, we passed our favorite pizza restaurant: closed. The toy store: closed. The diner where we often went for brunch on Saturdays: closed. The fabric store: closed. The coffee shop: closed. I thought of my friend who owns a restaurant in the town next to ours. The business had been struggling financially before the crisis, and my friend had a new baby. I thought about my public health colleagues around the world who were scrambling to respond to the pandemic; I had spoken by videoconference that week to several coworkers, and we were all worried about the implications of the pandemic for sub-Saharan Africa and Southeast Asia. In the United States, two of my cousins worked in hospitals, and one had already tested positive for the virus. My godparents in New Orleans both had COVID-19 and were seriously ill.

Lying on the grass next to Lila, I read a passage from A. J. Swoboda's book *Subversive Sabbath*. Sabbath, he writes, "is not an escape from the chaos of our lives; rather, it is finding God in the chaos." Observing the Sabbath, he writes, means "taking a day to cease our work of trying to fix or control the world. We cannot 'save' the world. . . . To Sabbath is to crucify our desires for control over the world."

The Sabbath crucifies our longing for control. This idea contrasts starkly with the message I received growing up that it was, in fact, my job to help save the world. Part of why I became so engrossed when I began reading Christian theology in my early thirties was that the Christian story offers a radically different message. The paradoxes in Christianity perplexed and intrigued me. The last shall be first, and the first shall be last. God is both one and three. Jesus saved the world by willingly being humiliated, tortured, and killed. Jesus will return to unite heaven and earth.

That last one—the promise of salvation through Christ—was the one that both gripped and flummoxed me. I was hungry for healing and justice for the world, so I wanted to know, What did it mean that Jesus would come back to save us? When would it happen? Given how broken the world remained, how could this promise possibly be true?

During the eight years since my baptism, I had dedicated a great deal of time to disciplined Christian study and practice. Yet in moments like this—with questions about the mechanics of salvation and redemption still looming large—I felt like I was still in the early steps of my conversion journey. The temptation to believe that we can save ourselves if we just work hard enough remained strong. COVID-19 seemed a case in point. Globally, it seemed obvious that we needed to employ our best human skills of scientific reason, coordination, logistics, innovative financing, strategic decision-making, and ethical leadership. If we found and utilized better and more efficient technical and political solutions, couldn't we come a bit closer to saving ourselves and the world?

Yet Swoboda warns that putting our hope only in the power of human agency can lead to both painful and destructive outcomes. One is compulsivity. He writes,

> Because we do not often have any buffer against the distress of trying to care for the whole world, we quickly slip into compulsivity. Compulsivity is when

our impulses and actions become one—when there is no discernment about what we should or should not act on. Compulsivity is looking at the news two hundred times a day, sending texts with every thought, and getting work done whenever and wherever we are. But the Sabbath puts an end to that emotional crisis . . . by protecting us from being enslaved to our instincts and impulses. . . . The Sabbath is a boycott against human compulsivity.

His words rang true. Even though outwardly, society had dramatically slowed down during the pandemic, many of us were, understandably, more anxious than ever before. Perhaps this was the time when we *most* needed our desire for control to be crucified. Maybe the weekly boycott that Sabbath offered—not just from shopping or from working but also from our compulsivity—was just the medicine we needed.

The camping trip with Lila that month made me more aware of my compulsivity regarding parenting. We spent the weekend hiking and wading in a nearby stream. At night, we built a campfire and stayed up late. During the trip, I was reminded of a lesson I had learned as part of my weekly Sabbath observance: Sabbath helps me parent differently. When I let go of a preset agenda and make intentional time to be with my daughter and stepson, I am—unsurprisingly—more present with them. Even if I plan to spend "quality time" with them during the week, it usually involves bustling us off to some pre-planned activity. During Sabbath time, however, I let go of my agenda.

That weekend was the same; I spent most of the time following Lila's lead rather than imposing a plan on her. That meant that after she spent thirty minutes crushing chunks of clay dirt to make "paint," I helped her use it to decorate the rocks near our campsite. When she scampered up the steep bank of the stream, I sat nearby, watching as she proudly climbed her way to the top. I knew I didn't necessarily have to engage in all the same activities as she did; that wasn't the point. The point was about paying attention. I am usually busy multitasking while I am with her, and it felt good to set aside my phone and my pre-conceived notions of what we should be doing together. Despite the fear and uncertainty the pandemic had caused, the weekend together felt like holy time.

◆ ◆ ◆

Mommy guilt has plagued me since Lila was born. Although not acknowledged as an official psychological phenomenon, mommy guilt is commonly discussed in the blogosphere. One site explains that it is "the feeling of guilt, doubt, anxiousness or uncertainty experienced by mothers when they worry they're failing or falling short of expectations in some way. For many moms—particularly new, working or single moms—the vari-ables that contribute to this phenomenon are numerous and intense." Author Lauren Smith Brody conducted a survey of more than seven hundred mothers as part of the research for her book *The Fifth Trimester*. She writes, "As I paged through my interview transcripts, one word leapt out again and again: 'guilt.' The moms I'd interviewed had little else in common, actually. There were hourly workers and Fortune 500 execu-tives. Part-time workers, freelancers, moms on career-pause, adoptive moms, single moms. They all reported feeling guilty. So I looked more closely. Turns out, guilt meant different things to different women. . . . But none of these women, to my eye, seemed like they actually had done anything wrong."

Social media has turned the phrase "fear of missing out" into a commonly used acronym: FOMO. FOMO usually refers to the anxiety of missing out on social events or relationships when one sees others' happy images posted on Instagram or Facebook. But my experience of FOMO is connected to my intense and chronic mommy guilt; it's the Fear of Missing Out on the Fleeting Moments of My Daughter's Precious Childhood. I experience this when I'm physically apart from her and even when I'm not. If we're both home but not spending time together, I still worry that perhaps the precious moments of her life are slipping by.

I acquired this anxiety during Lila's infancy when well-meaning strangers would approach me in the grocery store, stare into her baby carrier, and sigh wistfully, "Enjoy every day. It goes so fast." When Lila was six months old, one of my mother's close friends told me that parenting would be the most meaningful and rewarding thing I would ever do, so I should make sure to treasure every moment. And of course, there was the common refrain I heard from nearly everyone in the early years: "The days are long, but the years are short." Collectively, this counsel made me paranoid. Was I adequately savoring the experience? Was I being present enough—both physically and mentally?

In many ways, this anxiety was counterintuitive because many moments of parenting are exasperating, boring, confusing, or maddening. Still, on the whole, I agreed that parenting was deeply precious and, of course, ephemeral, which meant that when I ended up being captivated by other endeavors inside or outside of the house—like having a demanding and satisfying career, or writing, or hanging out with friends, or multitasking at home—this translated into ongoing guilt and ambivalence. I was never quite sure how I ought to be spending my time. Part of me wondered if I would be somewhat relieved when my daughter did grow up because at least I would be released from the endless worry that I was missing out on her childhood along the way.

Making intentional time to be with Lila, like during the camping trip, brought some respite from these conflicted feelings. But the relief was always short-lived. When we returned home to our regular routine, the guilt returned. And in many ways, COVID-19 exacerbated it. Even though I was working at home because of the pandemic, the pace and demands of my job had not decreased. I had to participate in online meetings and calls; I had deadlines I couldn't miss. David was trying to shift his psychology practice to an online platform so he could do therapy sessions remotely. He needed to set up new systems to be compliant with regulations and to ensure he would be reimbursed by insurance companies. We were both busy, and we were worried about the impact COVID-19 was having at the local and global levels. And we still had to get dinner on the table and sort the laundry.

In truth, Lila was old enough to be fairly self-sufficient during this time. She contentedly read for hours and did artwork. She wanted my attention periodically, but she was mostly fine on her own. She did her online coursework, and we helped her when she needed it. She cried sometimes in frustration and due to stress about the assignments, and I was attentive and loving during those moments. On one level, I knew I didn't need to feel guilty. But I still did.

I knew I was not alone. During the COVID-19 crisis, there was a flurry of articles about mommy guilt in the era of COVID-19. Headlines like "How Coronavirus Exposes the Great Lie of Modern Motherhood" were common. Women journalists and bloggers wrote about their unwillingness to feel guilty about their less-than-perfect parenting during the pandemic, as they tried to monitor their children's online schooling while juggling normal work and household responsibilities. But many of the articles I read seemed to have an edge of defensiveness. Even if moms were *trying* not to feel guilty, it sounded like many of them did anyway.

During the pandemic, I found myself reading a short sentence from Leviticus over and over while reciting my morning prayers: "Six days shall work be done; but the seventh day is a sabbath of complete rest" (Leviticus 23:3). One morning, I realized that the statement offered a profound antidote to the persistent guilt I experienced as a working mother. I had focused so much of my attention on the Sabbath—on the day of rest—that I hadn't paid attention to the first part of the sentence. I didn't need to feel guilty or remorseful during the six days of the week I was working. Part of my work is to help care for our family and household, and I would always strive to do that with love and diligence. But my work also includes having a career, writing books, and contributing in our local community.

In Genesis, before the fall, God put humans in the garden of Eden to till the earth (Genesis 2:15). That means that work has always been part of creation, and it is good. Working—including working hard—is nothing to feel guilty about.

At the same time, we are called into relationship. Swoboda points out that the first time a "not good" appears in the creation story in Genesis is when God said that it was "*not good that the man should be alone*" (Genesis 2:18; emphasis added). Before that, things in creation were only deemed "good": the land, the water, the living creatures. But working alone was "not good." So God caused the man to enter a deep sleep and "took one of his ribs and closed up its place with flesh" (Genesis 2:21). From that rib—from the man's own body—God created a companion who is described as a "helper" as his partner (Genesis 2:18).

It is not good to be alone, and during COVID-19, a lot of people suffered from social isolation. In my household, I was lucky. There were sweet moments of togetherness in the midst of the stress, including opportunities to work side by side with my daughter as she did her online course work. We got in the habit of taking a walk together each evening. In those moments, as we hiked along the trail in the woods near our house, I wondered if the crisis would provide other opportunities to further redefine our family's rhythms of work and rest.

11

///

Challenging the Fallacy of Work-Life Balance

Reclaiming a 24/6 Schedule

S EVERAL MONTHS INTO THE PANDEMIC, I participated in a webinar intended to explore how the global
community could sustain critical health-care services for
adolescent girls and women during COVID-19. During one of
the presentations, a donor from an international aid agency
spoke, and she advised that participants embrace a principle
that is commonly applied in humanitarian crisis situations. She
said that we needed to use the time during and after the pandemic as an opportunity to "build back better."

I had never heard that phrase before, and I loved it. *Build
back better.* After the call, I thought about all the areas where

this concept applied. In the United States and around the world, many of us clearly saw a need to build back better when it came to large-scale social institutions—health care, the economy, criminal justice systems, education, the ways we steward natural resources. There was also a need to build back better in our personal lives. As part of this, I wondered, How could we build back better when it came to rest?

Perhaps the crisis could be an opportunity to reclaim a different—and ancient—understanding of how to achieve balance in our lives. As a first step, I wondered if it was time to reject a prevailing ideal: the ubiquitous search for work-life balance.

◆ ◆ ◆

According to *Forbes* magazine, the phrase "work-life balance" is googled an average of fifty thousand times per month. Yet some have become increasingly critical of the concept, arguing that the framework is both limiting and misleading. The phrase implies that, as an antidote to our own tendencies toward workaholism and the unreasonable demands of our employers, we must fight back by reserving adequate time and energy for the "personal" components of our lives: our households, families, health, friendships, hobbies, chores. But writer Maria Popova argues this juxtaposition is inherently problematic. She writes, "I have always found the notion of compromising—particularly when it comes to this unfair tradeoff of work and life—to be a double-edged sword of meaning: on the one hand, *a* compromise implies reaching a happy medium between two conflicting needs; on the other, *to* compromise requires the trimming off of excess in one area in order to alleviate a deficit in the other, which invariably means compromising—in the sense of undermining—the area deemed excessive."

Similarly, in his book *The Three Marriages*, poet and author David Whyte argues that whenever we neglect any of the critical parts of our lives—including our relationships with others, our work, or our individual sense of self—we "impoverish them all, because they are not actually separate commitments but different expressions of the way each individual belongs to the world." The result, he argues, is that "the current understanding of work-life balance is too simplistic. People find it hard to balance work with family, family with self, because it might not be a question of balance. Some other dynamic is in play, something to do with a very human attempt at happiness that does not quantify different parts of life and then set them against one another."

Another problem with the conceptualization of work-life balance is that it inaccurately implies that the half of the equation that makes up one's regular "life"—everything that happens outside of one's day job—doesn't actually require work. But of course, almost all parts of life require work. Marriage requires work. Parenting requires work. Getting dinner on the table every night, being present to family and friends, working in the community, exercising: it all requires time and effort. Even tending to one's relationship with God takes work. For the most part, this is wonderful work. Still, life requires constant work—and a lot of it.

So we must not act as though our paid work and our personal lives are dichotomous. Rather, the real juxtaposition should be between our work and our rest. And this is exactly what Sabbath helps us recognize. The commandment tells us that for every six days we dedicate to work, we must dedicate one day to rest. During the pandemic, as I reflected on how we could build back better, it occurred to me that perhaps this was an opportunity to start aiming for *work-rest* balance in our lives.

◆ ◆ ◆

Of course, God's commandment is not the only thing that supports the need for weekly rest. A. J. Swoboda points out that scientific evidence and Scripture conveniently align to support a 24/6 lifestyle. Research has shown that if a person fails to rest for the equivalent of one day a week, they tend to experience a myriad of physical consequences, including insomnia, irritability, organ stress, hormonal imbalances, and high blood pressure. This results, he writes, in "a fascinating harmony between biblical and scientific witness." Both God and science remind us that "we are finite, limited people." Why, then, do we so often try to push past these limits? Why do we often act as though we should not—or cannot—put boundaries on our work?

Part of the problem may be that, objectively, the quantity of our work—including the expectations employers put on us—has become too great. Because we conceptualize our lives as a balancing act between "work" and "life," we fail to recognize or appreciate how much work is required to tend to our responsibilities outside of our paid jobs. If nothing else, the pandemic revealed the enormous burden and unrealistic expectations placed on working parents. In the early months of the crisis, Pulitzer Prize–winning journalist Claire Cain Miller wrote in the *New York Times* that the pandemic exposed three truths about working families: "One is that parenting is not confined to after-work hours. Another is that raising children is not just a lifestyle choice, akin to a demanding hobby. A third is that working parents can't do it alone." Rather, parenting is a twenty-four-hour job, and it is best done in the context of a supportive community. But our employers often expect that we demonstrate "undivided loyalty," which includes being available to our jobs all the time, even during evenings, weekends, vacations, and holidays.

Given this, it is no surprise that many working parents—especially single parents—do not feel they can afford one full day of rest each week. But rather than accepting this situation as unavoidable, we must recognize it as a symptom that something is deeply wrong. Miller points out that at various times over the past several decades, our society has contemplated the possibility that "government and employers would help women and men combine work and family." Instead, "the opposite idea prevailed—that it was up to individuals to figure it out." American parents receive little support in contrast to families in other developed countries. Yet, Miller argues, our kids are literally the future taxpayers and essential workers in our economy. Therefore, on some level, we are all accountable to support families. If public officials and employers saw it this way, perhaps they would "recognize the need for things like paid leave, affordable childcare, predictable schedules, reasonable hours and remote work."

In addition, an important implication of an ethic of Sabbath keeping is that people need to be adequately compensated for their work so they can afford to take time off. In an article in the *Christian Century*, Benjamin J. Dueholm tells the story of Maria Fernandes, who died while taking a nap in her car. Fernandes, a thirty-two-year-old woman who lived in New Jersey and held three part-time jobs, stopped to sleep between two shifts at different Dunkin' Donuts locations. She died from exhaust fumes after a fuel container in her car tipped over. According to her manager, it was the first time she had failed to show up for work.

"The current debate over the minimum wage . . . is ultimately about whether workers ought to have time for anything but work," Dueholm writes. "Working 40 hours a week at minimum wage doesn't provide enough income to meet the basic necessities of life." After Fernandes's death, her landlady told reporters that she sometimes struggled to come up with the $550 a month for the basement apartment she rented. The painful irony was that because Fernandes worked three jobs, she rarely slept in the apartment.

Dueholm points out that "the idea that the price of labor should be allowed to fall below the cost of life's necessities is, among other things, antithetical to the ethics of the Old Testament." Indeed, a Sabbath ethic has had important, tangible implications for public policy throughout modern history. Dueholm writes, "The gradual abolition of debtors' prisons and indentured servitude, the imposition of wage and hour laws and the provision of basic needs at public expense—all this grew from the economics of the sabbath." As such, "it will take more than individual piety for us to avoid permanent exile from time's palace. We will need a sabbath politics and a sabbath advocacy."

The implications of a Sabbath ethic also extend beyond people to other species. Lewis Regenstein, president of the Interfaith Council for the Protection of Animals and Nature, writes, "Modern day animal agriculture violates core Christian values," including biblical teachings that animals have a right to rest on the Sabbath. My brother Chris is an animal protection advocate, and he has dedicated his career to reducing animal suffering in the meat, egg, and dairy industries. Underpinning his arguments against animal cruelty is his belief that we must stop treating animals as commodities and instead recognize the sanctity of their lives.

As we grapple with how to develop approaches to public policy informed by a Sabbath ethic, we can also make changes in our personal lives. A mentor of mine who is a working parent once told me that she realized halfway through her career that her to-do list would simply never be completed until she died. She did not expect her work to ever be finished during her lifetime. That was an important lesson for me as a young professional and working mother. We cannot wait until our work is done to rest. To save our sanity and to transform our relationships with God and our neighbors, it is time to reclaim the gift of rest.

But in practical terms, how do we do this? And perhaps most importantly, *when* do we do it?

12

Does the Day Matter?

Seeking Sabbath in Community

FOR THE PAST SEVEN YEARS, a woman named Carol has been my Sabbath buddy. I met Carol one Sunday morning at church during an Adult Forum class facilitated by our newly hired associate pastor, Sarah. Sarah shared that she is a champion of Sabbath keeping, and she wanted to dedicate the first session to the topic. I was thrilled. During Sarah's talk, it became clear that a few of us in the audience had particular zeal for the Sabbath. Carol and I made eye contact, and we introduced ourselves over coffee following the session. We decided to meet one-on-one to explore if we could support one another in our respective weekly Sabbath practices. Since then, we've gotten together every few months to talk about our mutual obsession: rest.

From the outside, Carol's life and mine look very different. A retiree from New York, Carol lives at a much slower pace than I do. She does volunteer work, is passionate about studying family genealogy, and travels several times a year to see her grandchildren. Yet even though Carol has plenty of free time, she finds that implementing a Sabbath practice can have unexpected challenges.

Part of this comes with the territory. Maintaining any spiritual discipline week after week, year after year, can be tough, and this is why we sustain spiritual practices in the context of community and continually ask God for help. Beyond that, an issue Carol and I have both struggled with is the question of *when* to begin and end our Sabbath observance. The message we typically receive at church is that it is up to us to decide. We have the discretion to determine when—and if—to observe a twenty-four-hour Sabbath.

Yet I continued to want more specific and concrete instructions, and I spoke with Carol at length about why it was so hard for me to accept the "anything goes" messages about Sabbath keeping. I realized my frustration was largely due to two things. First, the underlying hunger I had for rest was so deep and so intense, I wanted my church family to acknowledge and validate it. Second, it felt like the free-for-all messages about Sabbath keeping exemplified the broader narrative about religion I received when I was growing up. When I was a kid, everything was left to my discretion. Discipline wasn't even a dirty word when it came to spirituality; it was a word that was simply never used.

Apparently, I still felt I needed permission to rest. I wanted somebody in a position of authority to tell me that if I rested for one day a week, I wouldn't be failing or "falling behind." Even if my colleagues checked their emails all weekend, zipping off messages at all hours about new funding opportunities and asking for responses ASAP, I wanted both encouragement and authorization to live a different kind of life, including approval to abstain from work for a twenty-four-hour period each week.

But nobody seemed willing to give that to me. So I realized I needed to stop looking for external validation. I needed to grant permission to myself.

◆ ◆ ◆

Setting limits on work can have real-life consequences. During the week I was drafting this chapter, colleagues and I were negotiating the terms of an important, high-stakes agreement with an external partner organization. Negotiations continued throughout the weekend. If I hadn't continued to monitor and respond to emails during this time, we might have missed key opportunities.

Given the real-life risks involved with reclaiming rest, I knew I needed support. I needed guidelines on when and how to take a Sabbath, partly so I would have help setting boundaries in a world that never stopped.

These questions remained salient for me during the COVID-19 crisis. While millions of Americans were laid off during the pandemic, many other workers faced increased workloads: taking on the responsibilities of coworkers whose jobs were terminated, pivoting to virtual work, or keeping up production under partial furloughs. Because I worked for an international public health organization, normal deadlines and stressors were compounded by the need to rapidly respond to the challenges the crisis created. There were health initiatives to redesign, new grants to apply for, a million webinars to watch and conference calls to participate in, new task forces to join. The World Health Organization recognized that just as we were in the middle of a pandemic, we were also in the middle of an "infodemic." We were all on information overload. All of this was occurring on top of our regular day jobs, which had pushed most of us to our limits on a normal day. During COVID-19, the need and expectation to stay engaged and plugged in to work increased, just as our collective exhaustion continued to grow.

I still wasn't sure about the ideal *when* or *how* of Sabbath keeping, so like any good, nerdy Sabbath enthusiastic, I turned to books for help. I read how in early Christian history, the observance of Sabbath shifted from Saturdays to Sundays. Jesus was crucified on a Friday, and he appeared again "after the sabbath, as the first day of the week was dawning" (Matthew 28:1). The "first day"—Sunday—became known as the "Lord's Day" in early Christianity. People also started referring to it as the "eighth day" as an acknowledgment that Christ's resurrection marked the start of a new creation. In 321 CE, the Roman emperor Constantine legislated that Sundays should be a day of rest for all citizens, thus codifying the practice for mainstream Christianity. Yet despite this long-held tradition, dissent continues among Christians about when and if to observe a Sabbath. Perhaps most well known of the modern-day dissenters are the Seventh-Day Adventists, who observe Sabbath from sunset on Friday to sunset on Saturday.

In his book *24/6*, Matthew Sleeth addresses the question of when we should observe the Sabbath with some levity. He says, "Even if we knew the exact date that God spoke the universe into existence, we still wouldn't know where God was when he sat down for the first Sabbath," Sleeth writes. "Was he in Mumbai or in Kentucky? Did the first Sabbath begin in one of

Africa's five time zones, or maybe to the west in Manhattan? . . . Even if we could answer these questions . . . would we know when an astronaut in the International Space Station should begin the Sabbath?" Such arguments, he claims, miss the greater point that we are "supposed to stop one out of every seven days and mark it as a holy day." Sleeth says that, in his opinion, "it doesn't matter what you call the Sabbath—Shabbat, Shabbos, Saturday, Sunday, 24/6, a day of rest, ceasing day, or Stop Day." Instead, "what's important is the stopping."

Reading this description helped me relax a bit. I imagined God in the International Space Station and conceded that the specific *when* of Sabbath keeping would be considerably less important up there. In the previous months, I had begun posting about my Sabbath practice each Saturday night on Instagram with the hope that I might encourage my (albeit tiny) number of followers to all start observing the Sabbath in the same time frame. My friend Bryan from church, who was one of the few people I knew who had a dedicated Sabbath observance, was in Tanzania collecting data for his PhD dissertation. He replied to my Instagram posts with enthusiasm. But of course, Bryan was in a different time zone than I, so no matter what, we wouldn't be keeping Sabbath at the same time. Perhaps my rigid approach to Sabbath and community building needed a reboot.

Or perhaps it was time for me to really think outside the box. After doing more research, I realized that, historically, the Egyptian and Ethiopian Coptic churches had a different concept of Sabbath keeping and the Lord's Day. Originally, they observed both!

Historian Wilson B. Bishai writes that for several centuries after the Council of Nicaea, both the traditional seventh day Sabbath (Saturday) and the Lord's Day (Sunday) were observed as holy days in the Coptic churches. Bishai quotes the Coptic version of *Apostolic Constitutions*, an early collection of church laws:

> Let the servants of the Lord work five days;
> On the Sabbath and the Lord's day
> Let them rest for the church that they might be instructed
> in piety. The Sabbath because God Himself rested on
> it when He completed all the creation. The Lord's day
> because it is the day of the resurrection of the Lord.

Aha, I thought; now I might really be on to something. Part of the challenge within my own family was that for years, I had not been able to negotiate successfully with my kids or husband if or when we could take an intentional day of rest together. By Friday evening, we were all burned out on work; it felt natural to them to take Saturdays off. And no matter what, I could not convince Lila to do her homework on Saturdays so that we could have Sundays off together as a Sabbath. She complained that she needed Saturdays to decompress from a busy and demanding week; by Sunday afternoon, she had regained some of the energy and motivation needed to reengage with assignments. But for years, I had wanted to align my own practice with Christians who took a twenty-four-hour Sabbath observance seriously, even if that number was dwindling. But the results were unsatisfying. Not only did I still feel mostly alone in terms of syncing with my Christian community; it had not been a winning strategy for our family.

But after reading about Coptic Christian history, I wondered, What about taking Saturdays off as a day of holy rest and, separately, recognizing Sundays as a day of worship and celebration—that is, the day we go to church? I talked over the idea with my family, and they were supportive. The new proposal aligned with what came naturally to them anyway, and they were fine if I wanted to overlay a spiritual framework. Resting on Saturday was also a better fit with the rhythms of my job. There seemed to be an unspoken agreement in my office that Saturdays were mostly off-limits. But by Sundays, many of my colleagues were starting to ramp back up again on email, implicitly expecting responses before bedtime. So it would be easier to maintain boundaries if I observed a Sabbath on Saturday, went to church on Sunday morning, and then eased back into work and chores on Sunday afternoon and evening.

Separating the Sabbath from the Lord's Day conceptually might also be an important nod to something rarely acknowledged: going to church can feel like work. That does not mean that going to church isn't wonderful. During the pandemic, the thing I missed most in my life was going to church for weekly worship services. In my experience, being at church every week is beautiful and meaningful and connecting and enlivening and dozens of other good things. But it does require effort: getting up early, showering and getting dressed, showing up on time, navigating the crowd during coffee hour. Plus, Sundays are often full of volunteer responsibilities for churchgoers. There are meetings to attend, Sunday school classes to teach, homebound parishioners to visit, potluck meals to prepare. The day often doesn't feel restful. And the Sabbath is meant to be about stopping. Ceasing all work and effort. Resting because God rested. In her book *For Sabbath's Sake*, author J. Dana Trent describes a conversation she had with a local rabbi. He said that, for him, the thing that distinguishes Sabbath from every other day is that he doesn't need to shave.

Metaphorically, we all need a break from shaving—whatever that looks like for us. We need time to sit around in soft jammies, following a quieter, gentler rhythm to our day. Showing up for church on Sunday mornings does not typically allow for this slower, rest-filled pace, especially if you have to hustle kids out the door. This may be part of why exhausted, rest-starved people are increasingly not showing up for church.

During COVID-19, a friend at church posted a beautiful photograph of her family on social media and wrote, "We will probably never again in our whole lives have so many slow Sundays in a row. We miss being out and about, around people, and especially church, but slow weekend mornings with just Sunday School on Zoom and playing a recorded service when everyone is well rested and fed, and has full parental attention, is quite nice."

I heard that over and over. People missed church . . . *and* it was nice not to have to rush out the door. Many of us experienced the dichotomy. We were lonely for each other, and we wanted communal worship to get back to normal, but we also didn't miss the Sunday morning rush. During that period, I reflected on this experience and wondered if *building back better* might include making a clearer distinction between Sabbath rest and Sunday worship. We need both.

Each Sunday—the Lord's Day—is meant to be a "little Easter," when we remember, commemorate, and celebrate Jesus's resurrection. It is a time to come together in community to share in delight and gratitude, sorrow and healing. And yes, anyone will tell you that planning a celebration—even when it is a deeply joyous occasion—takes work. Even just going to a party as a participant can be tiring. Yet worshiping together is essential. It helps turn our eyes and hearts to something bigger than our own lives and our daily routines. It means pausing to see the bigger picture and to reclaim a hopeful, love-filled vision of creation, even in a world that is weary and heavy-laden with suffering. Going to church may tire me out, but it also fills me up. Perhaps this is what author and theologian Ruth Valerio meant when she said that observing the Sabbath together can help us live "resurrection lives."

So this left me wondering, Would it be feasible to have both? Might the early Coptic Church have been on to something that we can reclaim? What if we reserved Saturdays as a time of God-given, Sabbath rest and then embraced Sundays as both a day of celebration and a time to slowly reenter the workweek?

I began experimenting with this approach, and it worked well. The shift meant that Sunday afternoons and evenings were now dedicated to errands, chores, and catching up on email. Yet I tried to engage with this work in new, more intentional ways, typically with renewed energy from a day of rest on Saturday and a period of spiritual reflection and celebration on Sunday morning. I made an effort to maintain a resurrection mindset.

Indeed, this approach reminds me, as author Norman Wirzba writes, that "the activity of being a church, the work of discipleship and hospitality, is not confined to that one day." Instead, we must "view Sunday as the training ground that prepares us to go into the week and there mirror Christ . . . as we work with colleagues, raise our kids, care for our elderly . . . tend to our lands and waters, and do our shopping."

The rhythm of the new schedule also seemed to be working for my family. Once, I began the weekend feeling frazzled, with a long, unfinished to-do list trailing behind me. On Saturday morning, Lila was the one to admonish me. She said, "Mom, it's time for the Sabbath. Sit down here, and let's light a candle."

Lila had never initiated a Sabbath observance before. She lit the purple candle on our dining room table and traced a circle of smoke in the air with the extinguished match, saying, "Mom, look at this beautiful smoke ring. Come on, Mom. Stop and come over here. It's time to rest."

13

How Then Shall We Pray?

Cultivating Rest in Our Daily Lives

IN HER BOOK OVERWHELMED, *New York Times*–best-selling author Brigid Schulte coined the phrase *time confetti*. According to Schulte, time confetti is what we experience when we chop up our activities and days into increasingly smaller, more frantic, more distracted, more exhausting minichunks. Time confetti is the result of the hundreds of choices we made each day, often unconsciously. It is "all those stolen glances at the smart phone, the bursts of addictive texting and email checking at all hours with the iPhone, Android, or Blackberry by the bed, the constant connection—even taking electronic devices into the toilet to shop."

Beyond our relationship with technology, time confetti happens as we try to juggle childcare, work deadlines, and household and community responsibilities while also attempting to scratch out time to take care of our health and perhaps have a bit of time left over for leisure. Schulte refutes the critique that only highly paid workaholics experience time confetti, writing that the ubiquitous experience is not just "indulgent 'yuppie kvetch.'" Families of every socioeconomic status experience time confetti. As part of her research, Schulte interviewed working-poor immigrant families. She heard directly how these families "cobbled together two or three part-time, low-paying jobs to pay the rent. They lived in apartments with two or sometimes three other families. They couldn't afford child care and shuffled their kids from an *abuela* to a neighbor to a TV set somewhere or hauled them along to work."

Beyond anecdotal reports, Schulte summarizes research revealing that workers of every socioeconomic status in the United States increasingly report feeling "overwhelmed, in poorer health, overworked, depressed, angry at their employers for expecting so much, [and] resentful of others they [think are] slacking off." For Schulte, time confetti is the opposite of "time serenity": a life in which people find a "way to knit scraps of time into longer, smoother stretches to do meaningful work, spend quality time" with family and friends, and have a "space to refresh their souls."

After years of experimenting with a Sabbath practice, I was getting glimpses of time serenity. I had finally embraced and committed to a consistent weekly rhythm of six days of work and one day of rest. I had made Sabbath a personal habit. And I could feel the difference. A regular routine of Sabbath keeping had become deeply restorative. And my productivity had not been compromised; if anything, my focus, satisfaction, and effectiveness while I was working had increased.

Yet many days I still felt exhausted and frazzled. This was not surprising. I was working a full-time job during the middle of a global pandemic, editing my second book, writing this book, parenting a teenage girl whose mood swings gave me perpetual whiplash, negotiating roles and responsibilities with David, and trying to lose the five pounds I had gained during the first two months of quarantine. Beyond my mundane personal preoccupations, I was overwhelmed and horrified by world events. Reading the news, I—like many others—became despondent.

Emerging data showed that the pandemic was having a disproportionate impact on the morbidity and mortality rates of people of color. And as the death count from the pandemic skyrocketed in the United States, the country roiled in shock and horror at the violent deaths of Ahmaud Arbery, Breonna Taylor, George Floyd, and other Black Americans. Tens of thousands of people around the country flooded the streets in protest. The Pulitzer Prize–winning writer and critic Wesley Morris observed that the rage about racism and violent white supremacy was "strong enough to compel people to risk catching one disease in order to combat the other."

The grief, anger, and anxiety were tremendous, and more than ever before, I was reminded that our individual resources of time, energy, money, and strength—physical and emotional—were finite. Could we afford to seek time serenity when the stakes were literally life and death for so many?

❖ ❖ ❖

As I grappled with these questions, I thought about the people I knew in my own church and broader community who dedicated their time and efforts to fighting tirelessly for social and economic justice. How did they keep themselves centered and sane when the situation seemed so bleak? What tool did they employ?

As I considered the question, I reflected on the role of prayer. Following recent national crises, including mass shootings, politicians have been criticized for asking the public to offer their "thoughts and prayers" to victims. For many, this often seems like a terrible cop-out, a lame substitute for tangible legislative action. Yet for many people of faith, prayer and social justice work are inextricably linked. As Pope Francis recently said, "Prayer and action must always be profoundly united."

Growing up, I wasn't taught how to pray. As an adult, I adopted a daily prayer practice several years before I was baptized in the Episcopal Church. When I first started praying regularly, I had no intention of exploring Christianity in any serious way. Rather, my journey with prayer began when I signed up for a yearlong course that was offered by a friend for "spiritual seekers" who wanted to explore religion but weren't grounded in any particular tradition. We were invited to commit to a daily spiritual discipline of our choice. I selected prayer. I didn't have a specific plan, and I wasn't familiar with the mechanics involved. All I knew was that for years, I had experienced a growing—albeit ill-defined—longing for a relationship with the divine. I didn't know what the feeling meant or where it might lead, but I assumed prayer was a reasonable place to start.

Fast forward a decade. I now know that there are many different ways that Christians pray. In my own denomination, the Episcopal Church, we use *The Book of Common Prayer*, which includes the Daily Office with services for morning, midday, and evening prayer that a person can do with a group or at home on her own. The church embraces other practices as well, including meditative approaches like contemplative prayer. During the initial class, when I first learned how to pray years ago, I was exposed to another classic method. One week the instructor gave us a worksheet with a simple structure. It said that prayer includes seven key components: time for centering, thanksgiving, confession, intercession, listening, petition, and closing. Ever since then, I have used this approach. When time is tight, I can go through the seven steps in as little as ten minutes. Occasionally, when my schedule allows, I'll spend up to an hour using the structure to guide my prayers.

Before COVID-19 hit, I prayed each morning in my car, and it became a consistent time of rest and reconnection with God. I had adopted this habit when Lila started kindergarten, as we started getting up an hour earlier to hustle her to school. Suddenly, I found myself with a gap of time between when I dropped her off and when my workday began. Out of that gap emerged the *when* and *where* for my prayer practice. Over the years, I learned that in order to sustain a regular prayer practice, I first had to commit to a clear routine. Without that, it was too easy to slip up and skip it on any given day. The driver's seat of a car is not a particularly glamorous place to pray, but it was functional. And that's what was important; I needed a set time and place to keep me on track.

So each morning before work, I would park my car, turn off the ignition, and pray. Sometimes I did this at a park that I passed during my commute, but most times, I did it in the parking garage at my office. I wasn't self-conscious. I figured if a colleague saw me, they would probably think I was dozing off or that I had my eyes downcast looking at my cell phone.

Before I made a commitment to daily prayer, I used to think that "being spiritual" was kind of like catching a cold—it just sort of happened whether you wanted it or not. After I began praying regularly, I realized that having a spiritual life is more like getting in shape. You can't get in shape by just *reading* about exercise or hoping it will magically happen on its own. You actually have to exercise. Likewise, you can't have a relationship with God without spending time talking to and, most importantly, listening to God.

I loved the seven-step prayer structure because it provided me with a simple framework for conversations with God. I also appreciated that the structure allowed for creativity and spontaneity; I tried to allow the Holy Spirit to guide the pacing and content of the conversation each day.

I began each day with the first step: centering, which involves a time to get quiet and focused on God. I did this in different ways. Sometimes I would just start with a simple, silent hello to God. Or I would briefly contemplate the different aspects of the Trinity, focusing for a moment on the Creator, Jesus, and the Holy Spirit, in turn. Sometimes, I would recite my favorite poem to myself or say the Lord's Prayer.

After that, I would move to the next step: thanksgiving. I generally maintain that proverbial "attitude of gratitude" in my everyday life, but ironically, this was often the most difficult part of the prayer practice for me. I was confused about the theology of gratitude. I often wondered, What does it mean to be thankful in our prayers? I did not want my gratitude for all of the positive things in my life—my family, my health, my home—to be predicated on a comparison to all of the other people who do not have these blessings. I don't want to say to God, "I'm so thankful that I live in a relatively peaceful community because I know so many around the world suffer under terrible violence and oppression." What kind of twisted gratitude is that? Instead, I would try to focus my gratitude on the ways I felt God moving in my life. For the love I experienced with family and friends. For the natural beauty in the world. For the difficult situations that held unexpected glimmers of grace.

After a time of gratitude in my prayers, I would move to the next step: a time of confession. According to Christian teaching, a dedicated time of self-reflection and repentance is essential. This step became a time to recognize and name my brokenness and shortcomings. As a new Christian, I was also confused by the idea of sin. During this period in my prayers, I would try to remember words we use in the Episcopal Church as part of Penitential Order: Rite One—"We confess that we have sinned against you, in thought, word, and deed, by what we have done, and by what we have left undone. We have not loved you with our whole heart; we have not loved our neighbors as ourselves. We are truly sorry and we humbly repent." I would turn the words over in my mind. All of the things I had left undone. All of the ways I had not loved my neighbor as myself. I was slowly, over time, learning what it means to confess and repent.

Next would come intercession: a time to pray for others. In my first memoir, which focuses on my conversion journey, I described how I initially adopted a Jesus-infused version of a Buddhist meditation practice that my husband taught me called "taking and giving." As part of that practice, you imagine others' suffering appearing as smoke; you then breathe that suffering into yourself with the hope that the smoke will destroy your self-cherishing. You then imagine breathing out a sense of peace to others. I adopted this practice but with one important addition: I would imagine that Jesus was overlaid on top of me, acting as a kind of filter. Since the smoke of suffering would travel through the Jesus filter first, it was his peace I offered to others, not something I was able to generate on my own. As I was doing this, I would pray for friends and family members. Given the difficult circumstances I was often praying about, I was surprised that the practice would typically bring me a sense of peace, quieting my racing mind and heart.

After that, I would enter into the listening phase of the prayer. As part of this step, I adopted a *lectio divina* practice. *Lectio divina* is a type of sacred reading that involves listening for God's word by reading a short passage of Scripture—just a few lines—slowly and meditatively. Then I would "listen" for how God might be speaking to me that day through the words. Sometimes I would read the Scripture passage that was appointed as part of the official church calendar, but more often, I used what I called the Ouija board method of prayer. I would run my fingers along the edge of the Bible until I felt called to stop. The results from this approach were often remarkable; I was frequently amazed to discover how God seemed to speak through a short phrase or passage in ways that informed and shaped the rest of my day.

Finally, I would end with petition and then a few words of closing. Petition is the component when we are invited to pray for our own needs. During this time, I would often ask God to protect my loved ones, to keep them safe and healthy. I don't know if it helped. I was never sure if or how God responds to requests like that. But I kept doing it. And I was grateful for the chance to express those prayers.

Overall, I found that this structure provided enough of a container for my prayers that I was not floundering all on my own; at the same time, within each step, there was plenty of room for flexibility, authenticity, and unexpected conversations and connections with God.

But then, even though I had maintained this prayer practice for many years, my daily commitment to prayer faltered during the pandemic. Because I was working from home, I was no longer commuting to my office, so I fell out of my regular routine. On one hand, I had even more time in my schedule than usual; I wasn't spending an hour and a half each day battling traffic. Yet without the typical morning structure, my discipline waned. I found myself getting lazy in my relationship with God.

As I became aware of this, I contemplated Schulte's insights about how we can move from time confetti to time serenity. After studying people from all walks of life and how they respond to stress, Schulte ends her book by concluding that, on some level, our experience of being overwhelmed will never fully dissipate. But through contemplative practices like meditation and prayer, we can change our relationship to the overwhelm. Without doing that, Schulte says, we risk treating life as if it is a "problem to be solved rather than a mystery to be lived." I noticed that tendency myself. I was becoming acutely aware that I often viewed life as a problem to be solved instead of a gift from God to be treasured. As I considered how to change this, I knew that recommitting to my daily prayer practice was critical. I also knew I needed to make another change. It was a simple step but a nearly impossible one: I needed to put down my phone.

14

Phones Down, Heads Up

Experimenting with Digital Fasts and Walking

RESEARCH SHOWS THAT THE AVERAGE office worker receives an estimated 120 emails per day. It is a deluge of communication. Reading about this reminded me of a conversation I had with Sarah, one of the priests at my church, about Sabbath keeping and rest. I was still hungrily searching for rules about how to *do* Sabbath. In her wisdom, Sarah wouldn't give me hard and fast instructions; she knew this could easily slip into legalism. At the same time, she tried to hear the deeper need behind my words.

"It seems like you're trying to create a barrier against work," she said with a penetrating look. "Your work sounds like a tsunami. And you're trying to build a dam to keep it back. You want the Sabbath to be that barrier, but maybe you need to focus more on what's happening on the other side of the dam."

She was right. I needed help setting limits. And on a practical level, much of what causes me to feel so constantly overwhelmed at work is the task of managing email. On one hand, reading, processing, and responding to email is an integral part of my work. I collaborate with colleagues all around the world, and email is often an efficient way to exchange ideas, information, updates, instructions, and requests. Beyond that, a key component of my job is making connections. I create linkages among people, ideas, projects, and strategies. In all of this, email is a tool that helps rapidly and efficiently connect the dots. Making these types of connections is not peripheral to my job; it *is* my job.

Yet the time and energy required to manage the voluminous amount of email I receive every day is the primary obstacle to achieving the kind of sustained, creative, focused concentration that author and computer science professor Cal Newport refers to as "deep work." Email is both the biggest help and the biggest hindrance to my productivity.

Beyond email, there is also my relationship with social media. I am active on Facebook, Twitter, Instagram, and LinkedIn. I frequently check these various platforms throughout the day, and not just for recreation. Engaging on social media has become an important part of my job; increasingly, I obtain valuable work-related updates on social media platforms. I often wouldn't have access to information posted by global leaders in my field if I weren't following them online. Social media has also become a way to help advance collective thought leadership; people can participate in substantive discussions about issues that are unfolding in real time.

Yet a growing body of evidence warns of the impacts that this plugged-in, digital lifestyle has on our bodies, brains, relationships, and spiritual lives. Research shows that the ubiquitous use and overuse of smartphones for recreation and social connections unequivocally contribute to stress, poor sleep, and mental health issues. As Newport writes, "In an open marketplace for attention, darker emotions attract more eyeballs than positive and constructive thoughts. For heavy internet users, the constant exposure to this darkness can become a source of draining negativity—a steep price that many don't even realize they're paying to support their compulsive connectivity."

For me, there is another, perhaps related and more concerning, problem. Over time, I have found that the continuous onslaught of email and social media content has become an impediment to my efforts to love my neighbor as myself.

◆ ◆ ◆

During his public ministry, Jesus was interrupted by people all the time. He would be on his way somewhere and a person would interrupt him and ask him for help. As one commentator noted, "Jesus was so often interrupted, even his interruptions were interrupted." Yet he handled this with grace, patience, kindness, and compassion, typically willing to drop one urgent thing to attend to another and only later turning his attention back to the initial urgent task. In the process, he never seems rushed or flustered.

My reaction to interruptions is decidedly un-Jesus-like. After living and working amid a tsunami of communication over the past several decades, I am increasingly stressed out. As a result, I can sometimes be unpleasant to be around, snapping at loved ones or treating my coworkers with impatience.

But Jesus didn't live in the modern era. Might Jesus have been a tad more frazzled if, as part of his ministry, he'd been managing multiple email and social media accounts as well as a constant stream of instant messages and texts?

I am not sure about Jesus, but the trend suggests that, increasingly, Americans are seeking ways to set boundaries at work and online, both as individuals and within institutions. Books like Catherine Price's *How to Break Up with Your Phone* attempt to teach healthier phone habits. Companies are starting to experiment with "structured disengagement," in which leaders within organizations prohibit after-hours work, including the use of email. Increasingly, there have been calls for digital Sabbaths and social media fasts.

As I experimented with abstaining from email and social media use as part of my own Sabbath keeping, I discovered that to have a bigger impact, I needed to do more than simply turn off my phone. I had to physically remove it from my presence. It turns out this practice is evidence based. A recent study found that even if a person's phone is turned off, having it in the same room "reduces available cognitive capacity." In other words, just the presence of our cell phones creates a sort of "brain drain." So at the start of each Sabbath, I would place my phone in a drawer in a room downstairs (not in our bedroom, where I usually kept it at night). Once it was tucked away, I often felt a palpable sense of relief. Only with the phone gone do I fully comprehend what a grip it holds on my mind and life.

Ultimately, I've realized that abstaining from email and social media is a practice in humility. We want to be relevant and important and be perceived that way by others. But this can so often be an exercise in pride. Quaker teacher and author Thomas Kelly wrote, "How slick and weasel-like is self-pride! . . . Our desire to be known and approved by others, to have heads nod approvingly about us behind our backs . . . gives us secret pleasures which we scarcely own to ourselves, yet thrive upon." Instead, Kelley invites us to cultivate "Godward-directed minds."

I want to cultivate a God-directed mind, but during the week, I find myself becoming so easily distracted, particularly as I read the news. Again, my phone compounds the problem; swiping compulsively from article to article generally only fuels my anxiety rather than increasing my insight, compassion, or trust in God. When I use my downtime to quickly skim news articles about catastrophic events on the small screen in my hand, it is easy to feel a growing sense of despair.

Given this, during my weekly Sabbath observance, I opt to read the news only in print form. I try to read articles carefully and thoughtfully, often "praying the news," as it is commonly called. As commentator Inge Schmidt writes, when we "bring our sincere prayers—our heartfelt desire to witness the spiritual reality that underlies existence—to bear on the act of following the news, we are changed. We are less subject to the ups and downs of the news cycle, no longer easily swayed by the currents of emotion that accompany particular stories and events."

In this process, as I worked to get my screen time under control, I thought about the Prophet Elijah's experience of listening to God in the wilderness. Fleeing hostile enemies, Elijah was exhausted and afraid. After traveling for hours, he lay down to rest under a tree and fell asleep. An angel woke him up and fed him, saying, "Get up and eat, otherwise the journey will be too much for you" (1 Kings 19:7). Then the Lord told him, "Go out and stand on the mountain . . . for the Lord is about to pass by." As Elijah was standing there, a huge wind came, but Elijah found that "the Lord was not in the wind." Then an earthquake came, but "the Lord was not in the earthquake." Then a fire, "but the Lord was not in the fire." After that, "a sound of sheer silence" (1 Kings 19:11–12). It was finally in this silence that Elijah heard the voice of God.

We must cultivate silence in our lives so that we can listen for the ways God may be speaking to us. As Abraham J. Herschel writes in his classic book *The Sabbath*, "It is one thing to race or be driven by the vicissitudes that menace life, and another thing to stand still and embrace the presence of an eternal moment." I knew that making time and space for this kind of stillness was essential. My life and my head were still way too noisy. A practice of digital fasting helped, but I knew there was another step I needed to make—literally. My life had become increasingly sedentary. I needed to get moving.

◆ ◆ ◆

During the fall before COVID-19 hit, at our congregation's annual meeting, the rector gave an update about our church's programs and finances. He noted that attendance at worship services was down, linking the pattern in our parish to a consistent downward trend in mainline Protestant denominations across the country. He cited an example of a couple in the church who told him they had decided to stop attending services on Sundays because it was the only time they had together during the busy week, and they liked to walk their dogs together in the morning.

The rector didn't say much more about the dog-walking couple, but after the meeting, I couldn't stop thinking about them. What did their situation say about the status of our physical, emotional, and spiritual lives? It seemed that the couple was longing for two things: leisurely family time and exercise.

During that period, I sometimes took a yoga class at the local YMCA on Thursday evenings, and the instructor would encourage us to make sure we balanced our stretching exercises with deep rest. He said, "Our tendency is to work and then keep working. But it is important to remember that without rest, the work suffers." Hearing this, I wondered, Why is this kind of message about work-rest balance so clearly communicated in yoga class but so often absent from discussions at church?

In an increasingly sedentary world, practices like yoga that fuse physical exercise with spiritual awareness are increasingly popular. The number of Americans who practice yoga increased from an estimated twenty million in 2012 to thirty-seven million in 2016. While it may be tempting for the church to dismiss this trend, people are voting with their feet, and it is important to pay attention.

Indeed, I recognize the need in myself to have more embodied spiritual practices. One month my Sabbath buddy, Carol, and I decided to experiment with this. We met on a Sunday morning in the church parking lot for a quiet, hour-long walk together before the ten o'clock worship service. As we were leaving the parking lot with our sneakers on, another parishioner saw us. "Oh, that's a good idea!" she exclaimed. The woman's instinctive response made me wonder if an intentional, community-based practice of walking meditation could be widely embraced as part of a Christian Sabbath practice.

Then after COVID-19 hit, one of the "silver linings" seemed to be that people started walking a lot more. I saw people walking everywhere. Families, individuals, kids, teenagers, adults.

The gyms were all closed, so people had no choice. They hit the streets and the trails.

On my own street, I was delighted when a group of neighbors created a series of interconnected pathways in a small patch of unused, scrubby woods. The area was meant to serve as a buffer between the residential area and the busy street behind us. No one had ever walked on that land before. Then suddenly, neighbors cleared at least half a dozen small trails connecting various parts of the neighborhood to one another. As far as I could tell, this was an uncoordinated effort. I started walking there in the afternoons after I had finished work. One afternoon I meet a retired guy named Ben who was building a small bridge over a ditch so that we would all have an easier time crossing over that part of the trail. I found it very moving; in the middle of a global crisis, we were connecting to one another and to the land in ways we never had before.

This experience became an important reminder that our search for rest and shalom—the ancient Hebrew word for God's peace and wholeness—is a communal journey, not an individual one. As author Verna J. Dozier wrote, Jesus taught that "the coming kingdom of God was to consist of a community of people who would find one another in love." Yet too often the church has distorted Jesus's message and "narrowed it from a call to transform the world to a call to save the souls of individuals."

Indeed, when Jesus gave his first recorded sermon in Luke's Gospel, he read from the scroll of the Prophet Isaiah. He said, "The Spirit of the Lord is upon me, because he has anointed me to bring good news to the poor. He has sent me to proclaim release to the captives and recovery of sight to the blind, to let the oppressed go free" (Luke 4:18) Jesus then tells the people gathered, "Today this scripture has been fulfilled in your hearing" (Luke 4:21).

I so deeply wanted to believe Jesus's proclamation. I ached for it to be true. I wanted to rest in the promise and hope he offers. Yet during the pandemic, I continued to agonize about if and how I could put my trust in God when enormous suffering and injustice persisted. The central question remained: How can we rest when there is so much urgent work to be done?

Without having a better answer to this question, I knew I would remain restless. I needed to know, Where does our labor end and God's work begin?

Part IV

SABBATH HOPE

15

Becoming Bilingual

Fluency in the Language of Faith

THE VIOLENT DEATHS OF BLACK Americans—including George Floyd, Ahmaud Arbery, and Breonna Taylor—in the spring of 2020 illuminated the painful truth that reclaiming rest is a privilege that many are systematically denied. Arbery was jogging when he was chased down and shot to death by white men in Georgia. Taylor was sleeping when police officers entered her apartment without warning, just after midnight, because they suspected two men of storing drugs there. In a column for the *New York Times*, Wesley Morris asked why white Americans still won't allow Black people to "run for leisure and sleep for rest."

As the death count continued to grow—both because of the virus and because of the violence in the streets—I was haunted by the questions, Would God really show up to redeem the world? And if so, how and when?

Ten days after George Floyd's death, my family and I went to a protest in Chapel Hill organized by the local NAACP youth caucus. The main street in town had been closed to traffic, and the crowd filled both lanes. At the beginning of the march, the group knelt in silence for eight minutes and forty-six seconds to commemorate the time that the white police officer in Minneapolis pinned Floyd under his knee while Floyd pleaded for mercy, telling the officer over and over, "I can't breathe." He died of mechanical asphyxia, the medical term for being choked.

As we knelt silently on the hot pavement, I realized how long eight minutes and forty-six seconds really is. Bent there, I tried to pray, but I couldn't. My mind was racing. All I could do was repeat "Oh God. Oh God" over and over in my mind.

As we stood back up, the chants resumed: "What do we want?" "Justice!" "When do we want it?" "Now!"

After we gathered in front of the courthouse, one of our state representatives, a Black woman, stood up to speak: "I'm one of the few elected officials who grew up in Chapel Hill and is old enough to remember segregation," she said. "I remember the businesses that refused to serve us." For more than sixty years, she said, the song "We Shall Overcome" had soared over the streets of the community, and for all that time, groups like ours had been demanding justice. Yet the progress she had seen in her lifetime had been incremental and inadequate. We needed to do better.

I agreed; I just still wasn't sure how. Saint Augustine famously told us that we will never find peace until we rest in God. The thousands of protesters who took to the streets chanted that there will be no peace until there is justice. It left me wondering, How do those two visions sync?

❖ ❖ ❖

I was in my midtwenties before I read a formal definition of humanism. According to the American Humanist Association, humanism is a "progressive philosophy of life that, without theism or other supernatural beliefs, affirms our ability and responsibility to lead ethical lives of personal fulfillment that aspire to the greater good." Until I read an article about humanism, it wouldn't have occurred to me to think of it as a distinct ideology. The essence of humanism, I realized, was so fundamental to how I had been raised and what I had encountered in public school and college that it hardly seemed worth calling out. A humanist philosophy was, as they say, the air I breathed.

Of course, I knew that billions of people around the world adhered to a faith-based worldview, but in my social and academic circles, it was different. We were people of empirical and social science. We studied and discussed political theory, and in those conversations, theology never came up. Our heroes were the peace and justice activists of the nineteenth and twentieth centuries who had fought to end discrimination and oppression. My classmates and I conveniently ignored the fact that many of the activists we most admired were animated by their deep religious convictions; we were only interested in the concrete change tactics they used and the policies they promoted.

In college, I studied the sociology of health inequities in America, macroeconomics, and constitutional law. During my junior year, I took a world religions class, but it didn't occur to me at the time to look to religion for answers regarding how to solve our world's most pressing problems. I believed that science and policy change, along with the tools of collective organizing and civil disobedience, were the best options for

improving the world. Religion had no meaningful role to play
other than as a cultural backdrop that we, as social scientists,
should seek to understand.

Humanism promotes "the building of a more humane society through an ethics based on human and other natural values
in a spirit of reason and free inquiry through human capabili-
ties." This sounds reasonable and fairly comprehensive. So why
wasn't I satisfied? Why, in my early thirties, did I go looking
for more?

Part of the reason was because of my husband. As a Buddhist, David spends countless hours studying, teaching, and
meditating on the root causes of human suffering. In my
undergraduate and graduate training, I was taught to diagnose
underlying reasons for individual and societal problems, so I
was deeply intrigued by David's approach. David explains that
from a Buddhist perspective, we have fundamental mispercep-
tions of how the world and our minds work. We mistakenly
believe that all objects and experiences exist inherently outside
of ourselves, and this faulty perception results in emotional and
cognitive reactions of craving and aversion, which, in turn, lead
to nonacceptance and suffering. David is a clinical psychologist, and he once wrote a blog post explaining the differences
between psychotherapy and Buddhist practice, both of which
seek to transform the mind. He wrote, "Traditionally, the field
of mental health seeks to optimize the functioning of a self in
relation to objectively existing external conditions. The 'self'
is seen as essentially functional and . . . mental illness is often
conceptualized as an illness of a potentially healthy self." In
contrast, Buddhism teaches that the self is problematic and that
"self-cherishing is a fundamental delusion and cause of suffering." So what can we do about these delusions? When we're

able to reduce and eliminate our self-cherishing by cultivating a virtuous mind, we have the potential to be liberated from suffering and, in turn, can help others on the same path. This does not mean we ignore or minimize systematic injustice or oppression. Rather, it is an acknowledgment that permanent change can't be achieved without transforming minds.

Over the years, I have been deeply influenced by the teachings of Buddhism and the ways I've seen David living and modeling these principles. Yet the more I learned, the more I felt like something was missing. Before I began my own conversion journey, which ultimately led to my baptism and confirmation in the Episcopal Church, I could barely articulate the desire even to myself. Yet the longing was undeniable. I wanted a relationship with the divine.

The other reason I began to look beyond a humanist worldview was more concrete and practical. At that point, I had worked in the nonprofit sector for over a decade, and I was discouraged. My colleagues and I understood that systemic injustices existed, and we wanted to promote social change, but our efforts often seemed ineffective. In fact, much of what we did seemed self-serving; we worked hard to get grant funding so we could keep our jobs. Once our livelihoods were secure, we worked hard to keep our donors happy. This often meant working on activities that seemed to miss the mark of what people actually needed and did little to change the underlying systems that had created problems in the first place. I was worried I was wasting my time and our donors' money. More than that, I was worried I was perpetuating what David's Buddhist teachings would call self-cherishing; too often, my biggest concerns were about my own job security and reputation rather than promoting real, lasting change.

Then I unexpectedly encountered Jesus. When I was baptized in my early thirties, I wanted to take refuge in a Christian
worldview. I wanted to embrace a Christian hope.

But what *is* the Christian hope? It turns out that the core
message is more complicated than I would have expected. Part
of the problem, I've discovered, is that there are a lot of different versions of what it means to be a Christian and what it
means to put our hope in God's promise to redeem our broken
world.

◆ ◆ ◆

Theologian N. T. Wright, a bishop in the Anglican Church and
a New Testament scholar, writes about the meaning and implications of Christian hope in his book *After You Believe: Why
Christian Character Matters*. He describes two popular versions of the Christian story that, he says, get it partly right but
fundamentally miss the mark. For people who embrace these
close-but-not-quite-right understandings of the faith, he says
it is like they are trying to be Christian "with one hand tied
behind their back."

The first partial narrative, Wright says, emphasizes "the
idea of a disembodied heaven." In this worldview, Christians
view the goal as "the final bliss of heaven, away from this life
of space, time and matter," and living in the present involves
a "practice of detached spirituality." Since earth is just a temporary way station, human problems—including entrenched
suffering—are not of utmost concern.

This understanding misses the mark, Wright says—but so
does the other version in which Christians believe that the goal
of this life is to "establish God's kingdom on earth by our own

hard work." In this other framework, "Christian living in the present consists of anticipating the final kingdom on earth by working and campaigning for justice, peace, and the alleviation of poverty and distress." Although Wright acknowledges that this worldview has "plenty of 'good news' by which people can live," he also says that in this version, the "heart of the matter seems to be strangely missing—which is perhaps why the attempts to live by this scheme are never as successful as their proponents hope."

The second version aligns with how I naturally approach Christianity. It also captures where I seemed to be stuck. After nearly a decade of being a Christian, I still felt like I was missing the heart of the matter, as Wright said—not making much progress (whatever that even means). I still felt both restless *and* ineffective. A frustrating combination.

Part of the problem, I realized, was that I was still too focused on my own potentially heroic role in the story of salvation. The secular version of humanism I grew up with essentially spoon-fed me a narcissistic worldview. It put me—and other people too, but most of all me—at the center of the action. I was taught that through my perseverance, insight, creativity, and effort, I might help "save" the world.

Yet as a newly baptized Christian, I was learning a different and more nuanced understanding of how salvation is unfolding. In signing up to follow Jesus, I had agreed to place my trust in God rather than in myself. So what does this mean? And what do Jesus's life and death teach us about what our place in the story is? First of all, Wright says, the goal of Christianity is not individual salvation (although that's part of it), and the "kingdom of heaven" is not a disembodied, faraway place separate from our current reality. Rather, heaven and earth are intertwined and interconnected, and amazingly, the launch of a new creation was inaugurated in the life, ministry, death, and resurrection of Jesus. This new creation is an upside-down version of reality in which the entire world will "be liberated from corruption and death." As the Beatitudes promise, people who "hunger and thirst for God's justice" will be satisfied.

In this process, Jesus's death shows us that the "kingdom and cross belong together." But why? Why is an instrument of vicious torture—the cross—required to help inaugurate a peaceable kingdom? Wright explains that ultimately, a new creation cannot, by definition, arrive through any of the means we typically use in the world. Rather, the kingdom can only be established "by its proper means: suffering, self-giving love." This is what Jesus enacted through his journey to the cross and what helped launch a new version of creation in which the ways of the world are fundamentally transformed.

Similarly, theologian James H. Cone also argues that the cross and the kingdom are inseparable. In his book *The Cross and the Lynching Tree*, Cone draws powerful, painful comparisons between the meaning of the cross and the horrific legacy of lynching in American history. Between Reconstruction and the start of World War II, more than four thousand Black people were lynched in the United States, often in front of large, jeering mobs of white people who not only condoned the violence but celebrated it. In many cases, planned lynchings would be advertised in newspapers, families would picnic at the events, and photos would be taken and sold widely as souvenirs. Most white Americans fail to make the connection between these gruesome, horrific killings and Jesus's death on the cross. But Cone writes that "the lynching tree joined the cross as the most emotionally charged symbols in the African

American community—symbols that represented both death and the promise of redemption . . . suffering and the power of hope. Both the cross and the lynching tree represented the worst in human beings and at the same time, 'an unquenchable ontological thirst' for life that refuses to let the worst determine our final meaning."

Cone points out that many activists during the civil rights era recognized and embraced this connection between the cross and the kingdom, including, most famously, Dr. Martin Luther King Jr. In 1967, after King made his famous "Beyond Vietnam" address, he was widely criticized in the news media, by government officials, and even within the Black community. Cone explains that King was "under extreme pressure to end his opposition to the war in Vietnam and to tone down his fight against racism and poverty." Yet, Cone writes, as he "struggled to find his way forward, he turned again to the cross to deepen his faith and his determination to stay the course no matter what."

For King, social justice work and theology were inextricably linked; Cone writes that "nonviolence was more than a strategy; it was the way of life defined by love for others—the only way to heal broken humanity." King believed that "the cycle of violence and hate could be broken only with nonviolence and love, as revealed in Jesus' rejection of violence and his acceptance of a shameful death on a cruel cross." In contrast, some of King's supporters accepted nonviolence as an effective political strategy, but they "rejected King's religious faith." Nonetheless, King remained steadfast. His "faith was defined by the mystery of divine salvation in the cross and by the belief that Jesus was the answer."

Cone points out that "the paradox of the crucified savior lies at the heart of the Christian story." So what does this paradox mean for everyday people trying to live reasonably good lives and make a positive—albeit modest—impact in the world?

Often, our approach is to work harder to try to improve ourselves. We know we are flawed. We go to therapy, read self-help books, practice mindfulness, and attend seminars to try to incrementally improve ourselves. We want to become more patient, compassionate, kind, and skillful. And we want to be more *effective*. But Christianity teaches that any self-directed attempts at self-improvement will be inadequate. N. T. Wright explains that Jesus "taught that humans . . . have a sickness of heart which all attempts at betterment could not touch." Our sickness is so entrenched that "the corruption and decay of the old world . . . the habits and patterns of thought, imagination and life, had to be not just reformed but killed." And all of this—the corruption and sickness in the world and in us—is what needed to be crucified through Jesus's death. This is why baptism is described as a process of dying to self; when we enter the waters of baptism, we enter a tomb. In Romans, Saint Paul wrote, "Do you not know that all of us who have been baptized into Christ Jesus were baptized into his death? Therefore we have been buried with him by baptism into death, so that, just as Christ was raised from the dead by the glory of the Father, so we too might walk in newness of life" (Romans 6:3–4).

Fundamentally, Jesus taught that there is no place for the type of virtue we view "as self-made." Instead, our own efforts at self-improvement are symptoms of our most fundamental sickness: our pride.

Yet ironically, that form of pride—a pride in human effort, competence, ethics, and diligence—is exactly the quality that my humanist upbringing taught me to view as our most important virtue. No wonder I had trouble resting, and no wonder I was confused. For most of my life, I adhered to a worldview in which the responsibility for redemption lies on humans' shoulders, including my own. In that framework, rest is valued as an effective means of self-care that will allow me to refuel my gas tank and—as quickly as possible—get back to work. Christianity, in contrast, teaches that rest is part of a larger process of dying to self.

Both narratives held sway over me. Could I ever reconcile them? Was that even possible? And if I was going to rely on something other than my own attempts at self-made virtue, as Christian teaching instructed, how should I proceed? How could I unlearn my pride and hubris, and how might I learn to rest in the process?

◆ ◆ ◆

As I was working on this book, an image from the Bible kept popping into my mind, unbidden, day after day. Since I was not raised reading or learning Bible stories as a child, this was unusual for me. I was in my early thirties when I began reading the Bible for the first time, and even after a decade, it was slow going. So during those weeks, I wasn't sure why I kept seeing over and over, in my mind's eye, the four guys from ancient Capernaum who dug through the roof of a house to get in to see Jesus.

The story appears in both Mark's and Luke's Gospels. The incident happened early in Jesus's ministry. According to Mark, Jesus had just returned from Galilee, where he had been busy preaching in synagogues and casting out demons. Right before he returned to Capernaum, Jesus healed a leper who had begged him to "make him clean." Jesus did so but only after "sternly warning" the man not to mention what happened to anyone else. Instead, the former leper "went out and began to proclaim it freely, and to spread the word, so that Jesus could no longer go into a town openly." Jesus's anonymity had been compromised; after that, the "people came to him from every quarter" (Mark 1:40–45). It was as though the leper had alerted the paparazzi of his whereabouts.

As a result, so many people gathered "there was no longer room for them, not even in front of the door" (Mark 2:2). That's when the four guys who kept showing up in my prayers enter the scene. The four friends are carrying a fifth person—a man who was paralyzed—on a stretcher, hoping Jesus will heal their friend. But when they arrive, they can't get into the house because it is too crowded. So they look for another way in. They go up on the roof and "after having dug through it," place their friend in front of Jesus (Mark 2:4). Jesus is impressed with their faith and heals the man, saying, "Son, your sins are forgiven" (Mark 2:5). This proclamation perturbs the scribes who are there. Believing that only God can forgive sins, they consider Jesus's words to be blasphemy.

As a reader, I am less interested in the theological tussle that occurs with the scribes. I am more focused on the actions of the four friends of the paralyzed man. I can't believe they *dug* through the roof to get to Jesus. I admire their chutzpah, and it seems like Jesus does too.

As the scene kept coming to my mind over several weeks, I ignored it for a while. But as it kept popping into my thoughts, I finally started to pay attention. After contemplating the passage in my morning prayers, I realized I wanted to be like those guys. I wanted to do whatever it takes to make it to Jesus, even if it means digging through a rooftop without an invitation. Even if it means risking being perceived as rude, pushy, or over the top. Even if it means injuring myself slightly as I crash, with my friends, through dust and debris on the way down. Even if I have to squeeze into a small corner in a crowded, overpacked room, I want to claim a space near him.

As I continued to contemplate the image, I began to visualize what would happen once I landed in the room. I imagined Jesus telling me—somewhat sternly but also with love—to take a seat. In my prayers, I listened, sliding my back down the wall until I was seated on the floor. In my imagination, I looked around, loosely aware of other people in the room and how Jesus patiently tended to each one, listening to, diagnosing, and addressing their needs. Over the days, as I kept praying, I imagined Jesus starting to give me a few simple instructions. Mostly, my task was to make tea for the visitors. Some days Jesus's sternness returned, and he told me to take a break. Then I would wander around the small house until I found a thin mattress in a side room where I could lie down. Overall, the jobs Jesus gave me were not taxing: making tea and resting. Not saving the world, and not even really participating in the healing in any substantial way. That was Jesus's job. I was not running the show.

During those weeks, I talked with a mentor on the phone and lamented my ongoing confusion about Christian theology. "I don't get it!" I complained. "I'm *trying* to understand. How will the world be saved? Is God going to swoop in at some point and wave a magic wand, and then suddenly, the world will all be fixed? That just doesn't make any sense!"

I told my mentor how hard I was trying to embrace a Christian worldview, but I was becoming increasingly frustrated. I felt like I was squeezing the theological ideas as hard as I could, hoping they would form themselves into a hard nugget of truth that I could hold on to. But I wasn't making any progress. Could I trust God? Was God really going to end widespread violence and injustice? The evidence did not seem to support this.

After listening for a while, my mentor said simply, "It sounds like you're becoming bilingual. The language of your childhood is humanism. But increasingly, you're also learning to speak the language of faith. Maybe you can embrace being bilingual. It seems like the world needs both."

Yes, maybe I was becoming bilingual. I remain fluent in my native language, and I reflexively revert to that as I try to make sense of the world. But my friend was right. While it was slow going, I was gradually learning to understand—and speak—the language of faith.

Best-selling author and poet Kathleen Norris describes her process of learning the vocabulary of faith in her book *Amazing Grace*. She says, "I remain vulnerable to despair, which, for me, is the opposite of faith," she writes. "For many of my friends, the opposite of faith seems to be intellectual doubt, which has ceased to be a major obstacle for me. Perhaps this is mental laxity on my part; I prefer to think of it as a grace of poetic sensitivity."

Maybe I, too, could release some of the tension and frustration I experienced while trying to comprehend the tenets of faith and embrace more of a poetic sensibility. Perhaps the lingering image I'd had of digging through the roof to get into the crowded house with Jesus was an indication that I was on the right track. Maybe I was starting to learn the true language of Christianity: the language of prayer.

Later that month, I went out on the roof of our house. My husband had recently cleaned the pine needles out of our gutters, and I was retrieving a tool he had forgotten. While I was out there, I noticed a soft spot in the middle of the tile. We have a flat roof on our house, and for many years, we'd struggled with dry rot. We had recently hired a guy to replace several of the beams and all the roofing material, so I was alarmed to feel the squishy spot beneath my feet. I made a mental note to tell David about it. Then, unexpectedly, I sat down right in the middle of the soft area. I hadn't intended to start praying, but it happened spontaneously. In my prayer, I imagined what would happen if the roof gave way and collapsed beneath me. I imagined falling through to our living room below with debris swirling around me. Sitting there in the morning sun, I laughed out loud.

I pictured what would happen next. After falling, I would stand up, sore but mostly unhurt. As I visualized standing up gingerly in the room with Jesus, the words came to me. I knew what I would say to Jesus if I saw him there, in that room, after I'd fallen unceremoniously at his feet.

"OK, Jesus," I would say, looking up at him, "I got the message. I'm ready to stop trying to control everything. I'm ready to follow you."

16

Seeking Synthesis

Relief from Having to Save the World

M Y MOTHER'S FATHER, BILL, WAS a rabble-rouser. A progressive liberal from the North, he considered going to seminary but ended up as a social worker. My mother adored him, but he was a complicated, mercurial person. Throughout his adulthood, he struggled with alcoholism. He was adoring and supportive of my mother, but he would sometimes fly into moody rages. My mother was never sure what to expect when she was around him. She experienced a complicated mix of knowing she was unequivocally loved by her father and feeling that she had to walk on eggshells when he had been drinking. And my grandfather was a terrible fit for my grandmother Cornelia, a genteel woman from Alexandria, Virginia, who eschewed any controversial behavior. My grandmother sent my mother to an Episcopal day school for girls and hoped she would join the Junior League someday.

My grandmother was disappointed. My mother went to college during the 1960s at the height of the Vietnam War, and she quickly became a hippie and an activist. "By junior year, I thought I was majoring in drugs and demonstrations," my mother explains. "I would call home to say that I had been arrested for civil disobedience and my father would say, 'Great!' while my mother was shocked."

Given their differences and my grandfather's struggles, my grandparents' decision to divorce was unsurprising, but my mother was devastated by their breakup. The world around her felt increasingly chaotic, and now her family was falling apart. My mother remembers getting off the bus one time when she returned home from college for a weekend visit. Her mother had sent her off to school as an eighteen-year-old wearing paisley blouses with wide, round collars. When she stepped off the bus, my mother was wearing a secondhand army jacket, a leather cap over her long hair, and ripped jeans. My mother told me the story recently: "I remember looking across the parking lot at my parents, as a single tear rolled down my mother's cheek."

After college, my mother's youthful activism ripened into a deep, long-standing commitment to social justice. She was recently interviewed about her work in a book that profiles older activists, *How Seniors Are Saving the World: Retirement Activism to the Rescue*. I knew all the stories, but I appreciated reading the summary in the book; seeing it all listed in one place was impressive. My mother's commitment to activism as an adult started in earnest when I was a baby. While she was breastfeeding me, she heard about the international boycott of the international food conglomerate Nestlé. Several companies, including Nestlé, were being criticized by the World Health Organization for aggressively marketing baby formula to women in developing countries. The formula was expensive, and women often did not have clean water to mix with it. For mothers who are able to breastfeed, copious evidence demonstrates that breastfeeding is a much healthier and safer option. My mother joined the Infant Formula Action Coalition and worked for several years to support and expand the boycott. During that time, she spoke to a TV news reporter about the issue. I was eleven months old, and during the interview, which was filmed at our house, my mother held me in her arms.

Throughout my brothers' and my childhood, my mother worked tirelessly on a number of important issues: criminal justice reform, nuclear disarmament, racial justice and reconciliation. And as we were growing up, my mother conveyed her distaste for any work that only provided social services without linking to a broader justice framework. She told us that we had to address the root of social problems, not just put Band-Aids on them. But she also recognized that meeting people's immediate needs was critical. So while she focused her efforts on advocating for sweeping policy reform, she also modeled more direct and immediate social giving. She collected hundreds of boxes of food to donate to the local food shelter, raised thousands of dollars for the annual Walk for Hunger event in Boston, and taught art classes in a minimum-security prison as a volunteer. She is in her seventies now and continues much of this work. My mother is the real deal. She is a social justice warrior.

But my mother's personal beliefs about God are complicated; she is deeply ambivalent about her own religious beliefs, and she handed that confusion down to me. Instead of a religious worldview, she taught me and my brothers that it was our job to make the world a better place and that if we committed ourselves to advancing social justice, we would have meaningful lives. In retrospect, it was a lot of pressure. Plus, there was one factor that made my mother's example even more complicated to live up to. She did all of her work as an unpaid volunteer. My father had a lucrative career as a corporate attorney, and when I was a baby, my parents decided that she would stay home to be with the kids. So while my mother was able to dedicate countless hours to social justice causes, she never had to make a career out of it. She never had to pay the bills.

In contrast, my brothers and I had to make a living, just as we also wanted to live up to our mother's expectations that we would work to advance social justice. But this led to the painful dichotomy I had experienced in my career. I simultaneously wanted to be a servant leader committed to achieving real, lasting social change, *and* I had a desire to achieve professional success. I was both ambitious and altruistic. While the combination sometimes worked, these goals often felt at odds. As author David L. Chappell writes, the duality seemed to represent a "fundamental conflict of interest."

And, most painfully, without a spiritual compass, I never knew when my work was done. This is largely why I went searching for Sabbath. I wanted something—or *someone*—bigger than myself to tell me if and when it was OK to stop.

This is why my worldview still felt fragmented. On my personal blog, I wrote about how I was living a "bivocational" life as a public health professional and a Christian writer. When I published my first memoir, I intentionally did not merge my two platforms, including on social media. Few of my colleagues knew I was a Christian, and even fewer knew I had written a book about it. I was fearful that if my colleagues knew I was a Christian, it might undermine the professional credibility I had worked so hard to build up for myself. My colleagues worked diligently to advance evidence-based public health interventions around the world, and some of these people were overtly hostile to religion generally and Christianity specifically, often with legitimate reasons.

But living a bivocational life felt increasingly disjointed and exhausting. I *wanted* to claim my bilingual status, and I wanted both parts of my life to be accepted. I wanted to be more forthcoming about my spiritual orientation, even in my professional circles. I didn't want to jam my beliefs down anyone's throat, but I wanted to be comfortable showing up in my workplace as my full self. Yet I was still nervous. I wasn't just worried that some of my colleagues or funders would reject me because of my religiosity, although that was part of it. I was scared because I wondered if I was aligning myself intellectually with a faith tradition that didn't make *sense*. This is why the stakes were so high as I sought a theology that incorporated a vision and pathway for social justice. I wanted an integrated worldview.

As I struggled to understand the Christian message more deeply, I was surprised when I read the chapter about my mother in *How Seniors Are Saving the World*. According to the interview she gave with the book's authors, my mother seems to have a clearer theology than she had ever communicated to me. She told the interviewers, "I think that I have a higher power. . . . And when I am involved in social justice work or in making the world a better place, I feel that I am aligned with the life purpose that I have been given by this higher power."

My mother also told the interviewers that the guiding principle in her life is the serenity prayer: "I would say that I live by the serenity prayer. And it informs me in many ways," she told them.

God, grant me the serenity to accept the things I cannot change, the courage to change the things I can, and the wisdom to know the difference: these are the words my mother lives by. My mother had told me over and over throughout my life that religion doesn't make much sense to her and that she doesn't really believe in God. Yet she prays to a higher power for guidance. She asks for help knowing when she should accept things that she cannot change. And she "definitely" thinks this higher power animates her efforts to make the world a better place, and when she works for justice, she feels "aligned with the life purpose" she has been given.

That sounds like a pretty solid theological vision to me. Reading the chapter describing my mother's life's work, I realized for the first time that when it comes to faith, my mother is bilingual too.

◆ ◆ ◆

While it was a personal revelation that my mother has more of a spiritual orientation than I had often realized, it is also undeniably true that her faith is, at best, tepid. In this way, my mother exemplifies a trend that Chappell, a historian, insightfully describes in his book about the civil rights era, *A Stone of Hope: Prophetic Religion and the Death of Jim Crow*. Chappell argues that there were two distinct intellectual groups involved in the civil rights movement. The first was composed of educated, white Northern liberals like my mother. The second was made up of Southern Black Christian activists. Although these two groups had distinct philosophical orientations and approaches to activism, history has tended to jumble them together. But this is a mistake, Chappell explains, because not only did the two groups embody unique belief systems; their impacts on the movement were vastly different.

Intellectually, liberals believed "in the power of human reason to overcome 'prejudice' and other vestiges of a superstitious, unenlightened past." Ultimately, they thought progress was inevitable because "the moral improvements of the world come as a function of increased economic growth, scientific discovery, and educational dissemination of new ideas." Over time, this "would lead white southerners to abandon their irrational traditions." The result of this was that liberals, "though sincere in their devotion to black rights, did not see any reason to do anything drastic to promote them."

In contrast, Southern Black Christian activists "were driven not by modern liberal faith in human reason but by older, seemingly more durable" beliefs that were based in Christian and Jewish theology. Most notably, they drew from the tradition and wisdom of the prophets in the Old Testament. Many of the Black leaders—ranging from highly educated clergy such as Martin Luther King Jr. to leaders without much formal education such as Fannie Lou Hamer—"believed that the natural tendency of the world and of human institutions (including churches) is toward corruption." This group did not believe progress is inevitable. Rather, they believed it was necessary to serve the same role as the biblical prophets and to "instigate catastrophic changes in the minds of whoever would listen." The goal was to "try to force an unwilling world to abandon sin—in this case, 'the sin of segregation.'"

In comparing these two groups, Chappell powerfully argues that the intellectual and spiritual momentum behind the civil rights movement of the 1950s and 1960s did not stem from the progressive ideology of the Northern, liberal intellectuals. Rather, "it was the prophetic ideas" of Black Christians that "made the civil rights *move*." They offered a worldview that asked for and inspired self-sacrifice. They taught it was necessary to embrace "otherworldly values to secure a brighter future" and believed the power of the Holy Spirit animated their work and gave them strength. Perhaps most radical of all, they believed in a "godly grace beyond their control, a grace that demanded humility and gratitude in return."

Like many of my peers, I have put both the methods and the impact of the civil rights movement up on a pedestal for my entire life. Chappell would likely agree that this is appropriate. He writes that while civil rights activists "did not win all of their goals, especially in the economic realm," the achievement of Black activists was indeed extraordinary. Overall, the civil rights movement was "arguably the most successful social movement in American history, one that has been an inspiration from Soweto to Prague to Tiananmen Square."

Yet Chappell's historical account also shows me that I have largely credited the success of the civil rights movement to the wrong intellectual and spiritual worldview. For the most part, the power of the movement did not lie within the liberal humanist framework. Rather, the principles and strategies of the movement flowed from a prophetic Christian sensibility. Indeed, Chappell concludes that the historical record of the role of the "liberal and prophetic ideas complicates the standard progressive narrative of civil rights and American history in general." Ultimately, he says, from a historical perspective, "what makes the civil rights movement *matter* are the prophetic ideas it embodies—not the liberal-progressive elements" it contained.

So what was my takeaway from all of this? I wanted and needed a theology grounded in the prophetic tradition of fearlessly naming and confronting the sins of injustice. As part of this, I needed a theology of work—and rest—that puts God's grace at the center of things.

17

Tearing Down the Temple Curtain

Finding Unity through Grace

I spoke to my cousin Laura right after she got off an all-night shift at the labor and delivery unit at the hospital where she works in upstate New York. Laura is a certified nurse-midwife, and it can be hard to catch her on the phone when she is on call. Laura and I had been playing phone tag all week, and she called me at nine o'clock on a Saturday morning. She was still at work, but her patients were all resting comfortably, and she had about thirty minutes to chat before she began her morning rounds. Laura told me she was sitting outside in the small garden adjacent to the hospital. She likes to go there during breaks and is typically there by herself. She said, "I don't know why more people don't take advantage of this amazing resource. The garden is beautiful and so restful. More people should come here."

I asked Laura how her overnight shift had gone. "Great!" she said. "We had two births. Both were hard, but the mothers powered through. They both did an amazing job." My cousin inhaled deeply and said, "Honestly, the whole thing was triumphant!"

Triumphant. What a word. A process filled with blood, sweat, pain, and tears. Ending in a triumphant new birth. What a metaphor. "Yeah," my cousin said, then laughed. "My therapist often encourages me to think of my work as a midwife as a metaphor for life."

I was still struggling to find a theology of social justice that made sense to me, and my cousin is a wise, insightful companion. Laura is a single mother with a demanding job, but she tries to devote what extra time she has to social activism. When she was in her twenties, Laura was arrested for civil disobedience at a protest against the US Army facility known as the School of the Americas, located at Fort Benning in Georgia. For over fifty years, military personnel from Latin America had been trained at the facility, and many of its graduates went on to commit horrendous human rights abuses, including torture and assassination in Central and South America. Typically, nonviolent demonstrators at the protests were not prosecuted, but that month, a judge decided to make an example of the activists. Laura was charged and spent the next three months in jail. Jails, which are operated at the county level, are often underfunded and overcrowded. They are only meant to be used for short-term placements, but the prisons were full at the time, so Laura stayed in jail for her entire sentence. In her letters, Laura wrote that the lights stayed on twenty-four hours a day and that the cells were freezing. Reading her letters and processing the experience with her afterward, I have never thought about jail or prison the same way. Even relatively short sentences sound nearly unbearable to me.

That day on the phone, as my cousin sat in the garden outside of her hospital, I talked about my ongoing uncertainty about the Christian message of hope. Can we really put our trust in God to heal the world? Or do we only have human effort and ingenuity to get us out of the messes we've created? And how does rest fit into all of this?

Laura listened quietly. Then she said, "I think you're missing one important element: the power of grace. We can prepare the soil and plant the seed, but we don't make the plants grow. That's where the divine comes in." She continued, "It's the same with labor and delivery. I can offer a mother help and support and comfort. I sometimes provide a medical intervention. But I don't *make* the miracle of birth happen. That's what it means to be a midwife. It means *participating* in the miracle, not causing it or controlling it. I think you need to keep looking to understand the role of grace in all of this."

Even though she doesn't identify as a Christian, Laura's words were full of biblical images: the kingdom of God growing from a tiny seed, a world groaning in labor pains, the importance of relying on God's grace through it all.

Laura's words also reminded me of Norman Wirzba's description of growing up in a farming community that observed the Sabbath. He writes that looking back, he is "astounded by the fact that family members and neighbors stopped work on Sundays. At most times of the year this was not a big deal, but during harvest seasons it most certainly was." Wirzba says he would have understood if his parents and community members were anxious about the very real risk of losing the source of their livelihood if the weather turned bad during the narrow window when they could bring in the harvest. But, he writes, fear "did not overcome the Sabbath aim of rest and refreshment." This is because "worry and anxiety would be byproducts of a fundamental doubt of the goodness of God, a suspicion that maybe God's grace is limited or not enough." Although Wirzba's neighbors regularly experienced crop failure and the illness and death of livestock, farming consistently taught the "beneficence of grace." The experience showed Wirzba that "authentic rest becomes possible even in the midst of harvest time, because it is informed by the palpable, concrete understanding that God provides."

Yet as my cousin pointed out, the one thing about grace is that you can't control it. It doesn't happen on a timeline or in ways we dictate. As I continued to seek answers about the true meaning of work and rest, I knew I needed grace. I just didn't know if or when I could expect it to happen.

❖ ❖ ❖

In the meantime, I continued looking for role models. I read about William Wilberforce, a British Parliamentarian in the seventeenth century who dedicated more than forty years of his life to antislavery campaigns as well as numerous other social reform movements. Three days before Wilberforce's death in 1833, the Slavery Abolition Act—which finally abolished slavery across the British Empire—was passed. This was preceded by the Slave Trade Act, which passed in 1807 and made the international slave trade illegal. Wilberforce was a driving force behind both efforts.

Wilberforce's remarkable activism is well known. What is less well known is that Wilberforce was also an ardent Sabbatarian.

He was a passionate believer in the power of rest. This was not just a private conviction; he took his pro-rest campaign to the public square. He rigorously advocated for the importance of a dedicated Sabbath observance as a central part of Christian discipleship and community. This position wasn't necessarily popular at the time. During that period, religious zeal was often looked down upon and ridiculed in polite society. Wilberforce risked losing personal capital by advocating for "the reformation of manners," including the need for communal Sabbath keeping. He also, of course, risked losing time; a dedicated weekly Sabbath observance meant less time each week for work. Given the incredibly high stakes—securing the freedom of millions—his friend and colleagues might have understandably advised that it was unwise for him to devote *too* much time to rest.

Perhaps Wilberforce viewed Sabbath keeping as a strategic investment of time. He suffered from health problems throughout his life, so a regular habit of self-care might have provided him with the physical and emotional strength to keep fighting year after year after year. But apparently, Wilberforce's commitment to rest went much deeper than that. He wrote that the Sabbath should be embraced because it is a day when "ambition is stunted."

This phrase captures the challenging, piercing meaning of Sabbath. Even as we engage in urgent and noble efforts to change the world, there is value in allowing our ambition to be stunted through the discipline—and grace—of rest.

My office recently sponsored a lunchtime seminar series focused on women's leadership. One of the prominent speakers was our North Carolina state representative—the same woman whom I had heard speak at the Black Lives Matter demonstration about her decades of fighting for racial justice in our community. During the remarks she made, her passion, intelligence, drive, and commitment shone through. I was impressed and was left wondering how she juggled her many commitments. During the question and answer portion of the session, I asked her if and how she achieves balance in her life. She laughed. "It's tough," she responded.

Then she thought a moment and said, "Well, I do observe a weekly Sabbath. That is sacred time for me and my family, for worship and for rest."

I grinned. My friend and colleague Maya—the same person who had told me several years before that she thought our generation would never figure out how to juggle it all—attended the session as well. I sent her an email afterward with a dozen smiley-face emojis: "It seems like we found our answer. We don't have to reinvent the wheel."

Instead, we can reclaim what was ours to begin with—something that has been part of God's creation since the beginning: the sacred gift of rest. In that moment, I felt hopeful that we can relearn and reintegrate a rhythm of 24/6 into our weekly routines. And perhaps we can also learn when it's time to retreat for longer periods to a "solitary place," like Jesus did, for stillness and renewal, even in the middle of a restless world that puts endless demands on our time and energy.

In the process, perhaps we can become better at modeling rest for our children. This is a gift and legacy we can reclaim and pass on.

Despite my passion for Sabbath keeping, I also know the practice is not a panacea for all our problems or the world's. In her book *The Dangers of Christian Practice*, Lauren Winner explains that while God's spiritual gifts are always perfect, people inevitably receive and use these gifts in damaged ways because of our own profound imperfections. One of the greatest risks is that our spiritual practices end up perpetuating systems of injustice. As commentator Mychal Denzel Smith wrote, "One woman's justice might be another woman's oppression." The actions and structures that allow me to rest may often—with or without my awareness—cause harm to my neighbor. And, tragically, a weekly day of rest has become a privilege that many cannot afford. The appropriate response, Winner advises, is not to abandon spiritual practices such as Sabbath keeping but rather to also adopt practices of confession, repentance, and lamentation. Winner explains that confession and repentance invite us to consider the ways we have turned our backs on God and the ways we hurt others. Lament allows us to focus on the damage that has occurred for which we, as individuals, are not directly responsible. Rather, Winner explains, lamentation addresses "the sinfulness of the world, the brokenness that we are born into and inherit, the principalities and powers by which we are trapped." Even when we observe the gift of Sabbath, we lament that rest is systematically denied to so many, and we confess and repent of our own actions that contribute to these inequities and injustice.

❖ ❖ ❖

Sometimes things become "sticky" in my prayers. When this happens, I feel inexplicably compelled to pray for a person or an image, and that thing sticks—sometimes for weeks, or months, or longer—even if I don't have a particularly good reason to pray about that thing. While I was writing this book, I found myself praying for my cousin John nearly every day for months.

When I considered the situation objectively, I knew that many people probably needed my prayers more than John does. Compared to many others, John's life is going well. He has a great career and a wonderful wife and two kids. He is healthy and kind and smart. And John hadn't explicitly asked me to pray for him. So I don't know why I've felt compelled to do so and for such a long period of time. But I did. One day I texted him to tell him about it, and his reply seemed frazzled and urgent: "Thank you. I need them." It was during the pandemic, and John and his wife were parenting two young children under the age of three, and I knew John was seeking tenure at the university where he works as a professor. Maybe my impulse to pray for him was based on a subconscious awareness that it must have been a stressful time for their family, or maybe the impulse came from a higher source. I'm not sure, but either way, I kept praying for him. And maybe listening to that call—a call to pray without certainty—was itself a form of grace.

About a year earlier, I had a similar experience with "sticky" prayers when I was contemplating an image from the Bible. I was reading my way through the Old Testament, and I was in the middle of Exodus when God provides Moses with instructions for building the tabernacle. Moses is up on Mount Sinai, and God tells him that the Israelites must build a "sanctuary" so that God could "dwell among them" (Exodus 25:8). God then goes on to provide *extremely* detailed instructions about how to do this, including the necessary dimensions, materials, and process for building the ark of the covenant, the table for the bread of the presence, the curtains for the tabernacle, and the vestments for the priests.

I am not sure why, but as I read through the pages, I became gripped by these descriptions. The pace of my reading—which was already slow because of the *lectio divina* process I followed—decreased even further. I lingered over the words, savoring and contemplating them. I had no idea why I found these scenes so compelling, but I figured the Holy Spirit had something in mind. So I paid attention. It took me several months to get through the next fifteen pages. I spoke to my spiritual director about the passages, journaled about them, and even made drawings with colored pencils of the images I saw in my mind's eye.

One thing that struck me in the readings was the colors that God told the people to use as they were making the curtains in the tabernacle. God told Moses, "You shall make a curtain of blue, purple, and crimson yarns, and of fine twisted linen" (Exodus 26:31). Likewise, the court screens were to be made from "blue, purple, and crimson yarns" (Exodus 27:16). The colors were always the same: blue, purple, and red, sometimes with a touch of gold. The descriptions felt sumptuous. These were rich, extravagant, saturated colors that God told Moses to use.

When I finished reading the section in Exodus, I still didn't have any clarity about what, if any, special meaning the passages might hold for me. It wasn't until a year or so later, as I was working to finish this book, that I felt an almost imperceptible whisper reminding me of the passage. It came out of nowhere; I hadn't thought about those sections in Exodus for a while. Then I felt an inner voice saying, *Look to the tearing of the curtain in the temple.*

I was familiar with the image of the curtain tearing; it happens on Good Friday, immediately before Jesus dies on the cross. The Gospels of Matthew, Mark, and Luke all include a version of it. In Luke, the author explains that at about three in the afternoon, "the sun's light failed," and in that moment, "the curtain of the temple was torn in two. Then Jesus, crying with a loud voice, said, 'Father, into your hands I commend my spirit.' Having said this, he breathed his last" (Luke 23:44–46).

Author Daniel M. Garner writes that the curtain is a reference to the veil that hung in the tabernacle and later in the temple. Garner explains that "the veil's primary function was to separate the holy place from the holy of holies" and that "this separation is at the heart of the entire priestly code." The goal was to separate the clean and unclean, the holy and the profane: "The veil, then, was a physical barrier that both represented and enforced the separation from the holy presence of the enthroned Yahweh within from Aaron and his sons—the violation of which brought death."

But then, in the moment of Jesus's death, the veil was torn in two. This means that within and through Christ, we are no longer separated from God. There is no longer a division between the holy and the mundane. The curtain was ripped from top to bottom, and the divide between God and us is suddenly gone.

What happened next? Each year, as we recount the story of Holy Week, we often seem to rush from Good Friday to Easter. In the process, we can miss the day in between that gets at the heart of how rest fits into the narrative: Holy Saturday. Joseph, the man from Arimathea who received Jesus's body after requesting it from Pilate, laid it in the tomb on Friday, the day of holy preparation for the coming Sabbath. A group of women followed him and prepared "spices and ointments," but they did not administer them on Saturday. Instead, "on the sabbath they rested according to the commandment" (Luke 23:50–57). We are told that the women did not return until the following day, the day of Jesus's resurrection, which was "after the sabbath, as the first day of the week" (Matthew 28:1).

So what happens in between, on the day that Jesus lay in the tomb? What is the meaning of Holy Saturday? In the Episcopal Church, the Holy Saturday service described in *The Book of Common Prayer* is very short. My own congregation typically gathers for a simple service at noon outside in the church garden. The collect, or prayer of the day, begins, "Oh God . . . grant that, as the crucified body of your dear Son was laid in the tomb and rested on this holy Sabbath, so we may await with him the coming of the third day, and rise with him to newness of life." Christian theology also tells us that Holy Saturday is the day when Christ descended into hell and raised many who had died. This "harrowing of hell," as it is often called, reveals that Christ's resurrection becomes "the triumph of all humanity over death, and of the Earth itself over desecration."

That day—Holy Saturday—seems to capture the heart of Sabbath keeping. We are deep in our grief over the brokenness of the world. We do not know the healing miracle of Easter is about to occur. We lack hope. Yet for this day, we stop anyway. We cease our work. We rest, and we wait.

And after that, God's grace breaks through into the world, in a resurrected life, ushering our world into an entirely new reality. The first day of the week.

❖ ❖ ❖

That summer, my family and I traveled back to Vermont. It had been four years since my brother Andrew's wedding. Four years since I had sat on the airplane and confronted the ways my anxiety, competitiveness, and workaholism were making me sick—both physically and spiritually. A lot had changed. Andrew and his wife, Eva, had since had a baby, their daughter, Maggie. In my own life, after longing for a regular Sabbath for nearly a decade, I had finally adopted a sustained weekly practice. I worked hard six days a week and rested deeply on the seventh. The change was palpable. I still got stressed out, but I recovered more quickly. I felt more resilient. And importantly, I found myself putting my faith in God's grace more frequently and more easily. Like the farmers that Wirzba describes, observing a full twenty-four hours of rest each week was an act of trust that God's grace would be abundant and that I could afford to stop.

That year our family had decided to drive the fifteen hours from North Carolina to Vermont instead of flying. The morning after we arrived, Lila asked me to go kayaking with her. I was still worn out from the long day of travel the day before, but I agreed to go out with her on the lake. We retrieved the boats and paddles and put on our life jackets. But just then, it began to rain. I ran into the boathouse and got two flimsy ponchos from the closet. We didn't hear any thunder or see any lightning, so we decided to go out on the water anyway.

As we pushed away from the shore, a strange thing happened. I realized that two-thirds of the lake was covered in rain, with clouds crowding down overhead. But about a third of the lake was blue, with no rain falling in that section. I headed that way. It was an odd experience. One minute I was being pelted by heavy rain. The next, I was floating on clear, bright water under a sunny sky. Looking over my shoulder, I saw that most of the lake was still covered by a curtain of dense gray clouds.

As I floated there, I thought about the curtain in the temple, and I considered my ongoing struggle to function as a person who speaks both the language of humanism and the language of faith. Sometimes the two parts of my life—the secular and the religious—seem separated by a great, terrible divide: two parts that can never be joined into a single coherent whole.

Perhaps the tearing of the curtain in my own life means the end of false dichotomies. For so long I had wondered if my religious and secular worldviews could ever be integrated. Putting my faith both in humans' efforts and in God's power sometimes felt incongruous. And the separation left me restless, without clarity about where I could place my trust. But I was tired of the struggle, and in that moment, I felt a divide coming down. I imagined the curtain splitting in two and falling to the ground. In that moment, the veil that seemed to separate everyday life and God's grace seemed to disappear. This tear felt essential; it provided an opening that would allow God's light to shine through more fully into all aspects of life—in both my work and rest.

This, perhaps, is the meaning of grace. As the veil comes down, we are no longer separated from God. We are no longer kept apart from the holy of holies. God is with us and among us. And even though we can feel stuck in limbo between Good Friday and the resurrection, Easter has already happened. The Sabbath—the seventh day—has taken place. Jesus rested in the tomb, and now a new creation, the eighth day, has begun. Jesus abides in us, and through his journey to the cross, he has launched a new reality where heaven and earth are like waters flowing together, inseparable. And God has sent us an advocate, the Holy Spirit, who crosses the water and fills our sails with God's wind, often moving us forward in unpredictable, often breathtaking ways.

A few minutes later, the rain cleared, and the entire lake became blue. As I rocked gently in my kayak, sunshine shimmered on the top of each small wave. I looked around. There was no longer any separation on the water, only unity. I leaned back in my seat in the boat. In that moment, I felt how tired I was from the long drive the day before. Floating there, I closed my eyes in the sunlight and allowed myself to rest.

Quick-Start Guide to Sabbath Keeping

Six days shall work be done; but the seventh
day is a sabbath of complete rest, a holy
convocation; you shall do no work.

—Leviticus 23:3

WHEN MY MOTHER LEFT THE church in her early twenties, I lost a connection to the spiritual practice of Sabbath keeping. Years later, when I was preparing for baptism in my early thirties and studying family history, I discovered that my great-great-grandfather was an Episcopal priest and a popular speaker and writer in the late 1800s. In his book *A Reason of the Hope*, he asks his readers to imagine if God did not exist. One of the consequences of a universe without God, he wrote, is that we would tragically lose "the Lord's sweet day of rest." He said this rhetorically; at the end of the nineteenth century, he could not imagine such a world.

Since that time, the rhythm of observing a "sweet day of rest"—both within our wider culture and within the church—has frequently been lost. So now we must ask ourselves, How can we reclaim an intentional spiritual practice of rest within our weekly routines?

Over the years, people have asked me what I do—and don't do—as part of my weekly Sabbath observance. I understand people's desire for more concrete guidance; a large part of what compelled me to research and write this book was that I wanted specific, actionable instructions for Sabbath keeping. So while I've tried to avoid being prescriptive, here are seven suggestions for anyone interested in adopting a Sabbath practice.

1. REFLECT ON WHAT COUNTS AS WORK FOR *YOU*—AND WHAT DOESN'T

After beginning a Sabbath practice, it can be easy to slip into judging ourselves or others for not doing Sabbath "correctly," which—as Jesus illustrates when he challenges the Pharisees' narrow-minded, rigid definitions of Sabbath keeping—is not the point. Sabbath keeping will look different for different people: the single person, the stay-at-home parent, the student, the unemployed person, the full-time worker, the person who is retired. Our approach to Sabbath will also change during different seasons of our lives. Each of us must carefully discern—with guidance from the Holy Spirit and with the help of wise friends and mentors—what constitutes work in our lives as well as how we can realistically carve out time to rest from this work.

Once you've figured what you *won't* do on the Sabbath, it is time to reflect on what you *will* do. Jesus posed the question, "Is it lawful to do good or to do harm on the sabbath, to save life or to destroy it?" (Luke 6:9). This is a good question to reflect on as we think about what activities we will engage in during our day of rest. Author A. J. Swoboda writes, "Our family has summed it up like this: Is the activity in question life giving, or is it life taking? That is, does it bring us life, rest, hope and wholeness? Or does it drain us, pour us out, stress us, or load us down?"

A good rule of thumb, Swoboda writes, is to consider engaging in activities that are not typically part of our day-to-day work. He writes, "Because a majority of my job is deskbound, I find that on the Sabbath day I need rest from my sedentary work by entering into some kind of physical activity." Likewise, because I don't engage in physical work as part of my day job, I sometimes garden or do light yard work on the Sabbath. But I bring a mindset of relaxed enjoyment to these activities rather than viewing them as a productive enterprise. Likewise, during the week, I often prepare meals in a rush; my goal is to get something easy on the table in the shortest amount of time possible. In contrast, on the Sabbath, I linger over food preparation. I cut vegetables with a sense of awe and appreciation for their colors, textures, and flavors.

I also try to avoid my typical multitasking. During the week, I often scatter my time and energy in a million directions, often resulting in what author Brigid Schulte calls "time confetti." Being more deliberate on the Sabbath can help us become more purposeful about how we spend our time and energy during the week as well.

2. TURN OFF YOUR DEVICES
AND PUT THEM AWAY

Consider using the Sabbath to reexamine your relationship with screen time. On my day of intentional rest, my laptop gets shut off, put into a bag, and placed inside a closet for a full twenty-four hours. I also turn off my cell phone during the Sabbath and typically put it in a drawer in the hallway downstairs. Importantly, I do not keep my phone in my bedroom, where it usually gets charged during the week. New evidence is starting to reveal that having our devices in the same room as us, even turned off, can create a type of "brain drain."

You may object to turning off your cell phone, arguing that emergencies can come up and loved ones might need to call or text you. But explore if you can find effective work-arounds. In my house, we still have a landline phone (shocking, I know!), so I inform my family and a handful of close friends that I will be "off-line" during the Sabbath and to call our landline phone if there's an issue or if they want to talk. I've also researched how to set up an "away" reply for text messages on my phone. This may require downloading a special app, but with it, you can easily create a short, automatic reply so that when you receive a text message, the sender will get a brief response saying you're away from your phone. Because people often expect a nearly immediate response to text messages, this approach may help you relax.

Beyond these concrete changes, Sabbath can allow us to deeply examine the role that screen time plays in our lives. Cal Newport, author and computer scientist, argues convincingly in his book *Digital Minimalism* that modern technologies are designed to be addictive, and we have to "move beyond tweaks and instead rebuild our relationship with technology from scratch, using our deeply held values as a foundation." Sabbath can be a time to get back in touch with these deeply held values such as prioritizing spending time with family and in nature as well as volunteering or exploring creative passions.

I keep a magnet on my desk that reads "She turned off her phone and lived happily ever after." This can be you. Allow yourself to find out what your happily ever after entails when your screens are off and your devices are put away.

3. CELEBRATE AND ENJOY YOUR BODY

In addition to examining our relationships with technology, our relationships with our bodies can also be transformed on the Sabbath. During the week, we often exercise because it is an important component of taking care of our health, but it may not always feel particularly joyful. Similarly, during the workweek, physical intimacy with a partner can sometimes feel like something we're too exhausted to consider. On the Sabbath, I encourage you to shift your perspective on all of this. A "Sabbath nap" in the afternoons (smile, wink) has been a game changer in my marriage (see chapter 8). I also approach exercise differently; Sabbath is not a day I work to change my body. Rather, it is a day to delight in the created world, including how God has and is creating me, right now, just as I am. On the Sabbath, I may take a walk or a hike or a jog because I want to and it feels good or because it is a time to connect with myself, family, or friends. Or I lie on the couch and nap because that's a wonderful way to care for my body too.

4. DECIDE WHEN AND FOR HOW LONG YOU WILL OBSERVE THE SABBATH

An important question is whether the specific day you observe the Sabbath matters. (Refer to chapter 12 for an in-depth discussion about this topic.) Whatever day you pick, I encourage you to try to embrace a discipline of setting aside a full day for rest. This is a somewhat controversial position among modern-day Sabbath advocates. Some advise that scheduling shorter chunks of time for Sabbath keeping is more realistic, and this may be true for you. And of course, taking time for rest, prayer, solitude, and stillness throughout the week is always wonderful. But from my perspective, part of the life-transforming gift and challenge of Sabbath is that we're called to keep the *entire day* holy. Given this, I have committed to a full twenty-four hours of rest for every six days of work, typically either from sunset to sunset or from bedtime to bedtime.

If you're not able to take a full day for a Sabbath practice, author Donna Schaper recommends imagining your week as composed of twenty-one distinct units: mornings, afternoons, and evenings. Then, she suggests, try to "set aside six units" and dedicate them to "spiritual leisure." Whatever day or length of time you choose, an important part of Sabbath keeping is making a clear intention *at the outset* regarding how long you will abstain from work and then sticking with it. Not only do I find the rest to be restorative, but the last hour or two of the practice often stretch me and serve as an important teacher. This time becomes the uncomfortable edge I rub up against. When I'm itching to get back to my email in-box, I try to push myself to stick with the Sabbath observance until the end. I'm often surprised and delighted by what happens when I do.

You may also want to find special ways to mark the beginning and end of Sabbath as holy time. Marva J. Dawn has some good suggestions in her book *Keeping the Sabbath Wholly*. After experimenting with different approaches, I try to keep it simple. I often light a candle and read a short prayer from *The Book of Common Prayer*. My favorite is "For Quiet Confidence": "O God of peace, who has taught us that in returning and rest we shall be saved, in the quietness and in confidence shall be our strength: By the might of your Spirit lift us, we pray you, to your presence, where we may be still and know that you are God."

5. FIND A SABBATH BUDDY

Maintaining a Sabbath practice can feel lonely. Sabbath keeping has largely gone out of fashion, including in many mainline Protestant churches like the one I attend. But that does not mean we have to observe Sabbath alone. As the Episcopal priest and author Barbara Brown Taylor writes, "God did not give this commandment to a person but to a people, knowing that only those who rested together would be equipped to resist together." This includes resistance against rampant materialism, exploitation of the people and the planet, and our own quiet competitiveness, hidden agendas, and unchecked ambition. These are the big "powers and principalities" that ensnare us all, so of course we need help resisting them.

Knowing this, when I began my personal search for Sabbath, I wanted to achieve a quorum. I wanted Sabbath to feel like Lent or Advent does in my church—that is, I wanted us to do it in the context of community. But waiting for a crowd is often not a winning strategy when it comes to rest. Instead, I found one person at church to be my Sabbath buddy. As discussed in chapter 14, my friend Carol and I encourage one another, discuss the challenges we experience, and remind one another to stay on track.

I encourage you to find a Sabbath buddy or a Sabbath support or reading group. The key is to find a person or people who share your longing for rest and who can provide accountability, resources, and encouragement. In my experience, this support can make all the difference.

6. MODEL REST FOR OUR KIDS

A friend once emailed me about how stressed and exhausted she felt, and I asked if she had ever considered a Sabbath practice. She wrote back, "Sabbath? Great concept. I'll review it again after I get my second volleyball-obsessed, tournaments-at-all-the-time child off to college in a year and a half." Like many of us, this person has to negotiate complicated family schedules and ensure there is adequate time for kids' homework and extracurricular activities. As MaryAnn McKibben Dana, author of *Sabbath in the Suburbs*, writes, family life can often feel "like a 500-piece jigsaw puzzle with 600 pieces."

In particular, Jewish and Christian leaders have often bemoaned the role of youth sports in undermining the traditional rhythms of Sabbath, including the ability of families to attend worship services together. The demands on families' schedules are very real, and it can be difficult for parents to insist on shared Sabbath time, especially as kids get older and increasingly control their own schedules. Yet I also believe it is imperative to model rest for our children. In my own decade-long struggle with clinical anxiety as a high school and college student, I desperately wanted someone to show me how I might live differently. Exhausted by too many academic and extracurricular commitments and fearful about an unknowable future, I wish I'd had more help and guidance about how to reclaim a rhythm of rest.

Rest is one of the best gifts we can give our kids, and as such, it is up to us to both model and set limits so that there is space for Sabbath time. This is not easy, and it will look different for every person and every family. Most of all, it requires effort and intention. This is why Sabbath keeping is a discipline as well as a gift. It took me a long time to negotiate a Sabbath schedule that works for my family, but it has been worth it.

7. FIGHT FOR THE RIGHT TO REST

The evidence is unequivocal: rest is critical, and it is lifesaving. As such, it is important that we fight to protect it. Part of this process is insisting that *all* have a right to rest. To achieve this, people need meaningful, safe work that pays a livable wage. We must work to ensure that all can *afford* to take a day off each week for rest.

This will require substantial policy change as well as changes in our culture. But we have a track record of this. Since our country's inception, Sabbath principles have helped shape legislation that has advanced economic and social justice (see chapter 11 for more on this). Part of reclaiming rest is embracing a Sabbath ethic that refuses to treat people, animals, or the planet as commodities. Rest can revolutionize our personal lives, but it can also transform societies, and our approach to economic and social change must reflect this.

We also need to make changes to the language we use. I have begun avoiding the phrase "work-life balance," which implies that our work and our lives are separate and that daily life doesn't require substantial amounts of work (which, of course, it does). Instead, I encourage us to reclaim our right to *work-rest balance*. I also no longer talk about trying to "save the world." Rather, I talk about *participating* in God's creation and in God's healing of our broken world.

In the Genesis story, people were put in the garden "to till it and keep it" (Genesis 2:15). This happened *before* the fall. This means our work is good. Yet we must always remember that God's creation was incomplete until God rested. We can't skip a day of rest and expect to be in right relationship with the created world.

Six days shall work be done, but the seventh day is a Sabbath of complete rest, a holy convocation.

Acknowledgments

FIRST, I WANT TO THANK my incredible editor, Valerie Weaver-Zercher. This book literally would not have happened without her, and I am tremendously grateful for her insightful feedback, skillful edits, and ongoing support. I also want to express special thanks to Kathy Izard; her encouragement and wise counsel throughout the project made all the difference. I am also very grateful to Erica Witsell, my dear friend and writing buddy; our collaboration and friendship for the past twenty years have meant so much. I'm also thankful to several friends who provided early review and feedback on the manuscript, especially Laura Gallaher and Tricia Petruney.

I have been obsessed with the topic of Sabbath keeping for nearly a decade, and I want to thank Maj-Britt Johnson, who first introduced me to the practice as a spiritual discipline. I am deeply grateful to Rev. Sarah Ball-Damberg for being a Sabbath champion and for discussing the topic at length with me over the past several years. I am also indebted to Rev. Dr. Clarke French for his theological and pastoral guidance and his review and feedback on the draft manuscript. Rev. Liz Dowling-Sendor serves as my spiritual director; her support, kindness, and encouragement during every step of this journey have been incredible gifts. I am also thankful to Rev. Gary Comstock for being a spiritual friend and mentor for the past twenty years.

Many friends, family members, and colleagues have supported me in this journey, and I'm particularly grateful to

Caroline and Brian Pence, Elizabeth Futrell, Laura MacCarald, Steve Erickson, Trinity Zan, Lucy Wilson, John and Brittney Holbein, Elsie Kagan, Wren Blessing, Kat Tumlinson, Mia Irwin, Christy Wilkens, Kirsten Krueger, Rose Wilcher, Sonia Katchian, Julia Powers, Bryan Dougan, Diane Steinhaus, Laneta Dorflinger, Rebecca Callahan, Allysha Maragh-Bass, Jennifer Ayers, Aurélie Brunie, Angela Conant, Eva Lyman-Munt, Tina MacDonald, and Kristen and Pam Rademacher. As I describe in the book, the friendship of Carol McGuire, my Sabbath buddy, has been invaluable, and I'm so grateful we found each other.

Brian Allain, founder of Writing for Your Life, is an incredible mentor and cheerleader, and I am tremendously grateful for the ministry he provides to me and so many others. I am also thankful to J. Dana Trent for our rich exchange and exploration of Sabbath keeping and for interviewing me for her book, *For Sabbath's Sake*; some of the stories in this book first appeared in those pages. In particular, I'm grateful to Dana for inviting me to be a part of her *Stealing Back Sabbath* blog series, where many of the ideas in this book were first explored. I'm also thankful to Patricia Raybon; our conversation about being "bilingual" was hugely influential and helped shaped the direction of the book's final chapters.

The seed for this book was initially planted when I wrote about the idea of taking a Sabbath year in my first memoir, and Elizabeth Turnbull asked me if I had actually done it. She commented that the topic would make a good book. That nudge was a turning point, and I am very grateful.

I'm also thankful to the WomenLift Health program, which works to catalyze long-term change to help women expand their voice and influence as global health leaders. Being a part of the WomenLift journey has been invaluable and allowed me to examine and challenge the limitations of the "work-life balance" framework more deeply. I am particularly thankful to members of my mentoring group and my coach, Monica Rivers.

I wrote this book as we were confronting what some have called a "double pandemic": the coronavirus and the impacts of ongoing racism and violent white supremacy in the United States and around the world. Like many others, these crises have caused me to look more deeply at my own white privilege and complicity in systems that perpetuate inequity and injustice. I want to express special thanks to Duke University's Decolonizing Global Health student working group, including Laura Mkumba and Yadurshini Raveendran, for their leadership in pushing the field of global health to look more deeply at our history and to encourage transformative change.

Most of all, I want to thank my parents, Lynn and Bruce Holbein, and my brothers, Chris and Andrew, for their unending support, love, and encouragement. My kids, Soren and Lila, are the best, and I feel incredibly thankful for them every single day. Finally, I am enormously grateful to my husband, David. His love, patience, wisdom, and support are extraordinary gifts.

When it comes to the challenges we face, my hope and prayer is that—in our work and in our rest—we can come together, with the help of the Holy Spirit, to build back better.

Notes

INTRODUCTION

1 *My colleague Maya:* I relayed this story during an interview with author J. Dana Trent, and it was first described in her book *For Sabbath's Sake: Embracing Your Need for Rest, Worship, and Community* (Nashville: Upper Room Books, 2017), 68–69.

3 *Extolling the virtues:* Lauren Winner, *Mudhouse Sabbath: An Invitation to a Life of Spiritual Discipline* (Cape Cod, MA: Paraclete, 2007), 10–11.

3 *Returning to a 24/6 lifestyle:* See Matthew Sleeth, *24/6: A Prescription for a Healthier, Happier Life* (Carol Stream, IL: Tyndale House, 2012).

4 *Deep, long-lasting effects:* Helen Lewis, "The Coronavirus Is a Disaster for Feminism," *Atlantic*, March 19, 2020, https://tinyurl.com/tl3pbbq.

4 *Health-care resources are diverted:* David Evans, "How Will COVID-19 Affect Women and Girls in Low- and Middle-Income Countries?," Center for Global Development, March 16, 2020, https://tinyurl.com/t54mp9x.

4 *Rates of domestic violence:* Barbara Crossette, "Across the Globe, Domestic Violence Rises as the Coronavirus Rages," *PassBlue*, April 6, 2020, https://tinyurl.com/y3y9a9dr.

7 *Long overdue awakening:* Justin Worland, "America's Long Overdue Awakening to Systemic Racism," *TIME*, June 11, 2020, https://tinyurl.com/y6sjqt2a.

CHAPTER 1

19 *For this generation of women:* Ada Calhoun, *Why We Can't Sleep: Women's New Midlife Crisis* (New York: Grove, 2020), 54, 8–9, 19–20.

19 *School desegregation initiative:* Kay Lazar, "Fifty Years Later, Metco's Dream Is Still Unanswered," *Boston Globe*, July 20, 2018, https://tinyurl.com/y2s34m58.

20 *There was a stark contrast:* Calhoun, *Why We Can't Sleep*, 46.

CHAPTER 2

23 *Intense pressure students feel:* Sara Rimer, "For Girls, It's Be Yourself, and Be Perfect, Too," *New York Times*, April 1, 2007, https://tinyurl.com/yypwpnq4.

24 *Something about the lives:* Rimer.

25 *Most prevalent types of mental health disorders:* Hannah Ritchie and Max Roser, "Mental Health," Our World in Data, April 2018, https://ourworldindata.org/mental-health.

25 *Reasons for this trend:* Edmund Bourne, *Healing Fear: New Approaches to Overcoming Anxiety* (Oakland, CA: New Harbinger, 1998).

26 *Structured disengagement strategies:* Kelsey Gee, "Sunday Night Is the New Monday Morning, and Workers Are Miserable," *Wall Street Journal,* July 7, 2019, https://tinyurl.com/yya7ybsv.

CHAPTER 3

27 *The ancient rabbis teach:* Wayne Muller, *Sabbath: Finding Rest, Renewal, and Delight in Our Busy Lives* (New York: Bantam, 2000), 37.

30 *Pattern of increased complaints:* Judith Shulevitz, "Bring Back the Sabbath," *New York Times*, March 2, 2003, https://tinyurl .com/y2xb7xc8.

31 *Aware of the lack of content:* As quoted in Neel Burton, "Man's Search for Meaning: Meaning as a Cure for Depression and Other Ills," *Psychology Today*, May 24, 2012, https://tinyurl.com/y92y8ogf.

CHAPTER 4

33 *Standing in coffee hour:* I first explored some of the ideas in this chapter in a blog post I wrote entitled "Sabbath Discipline" on author J. Dana Trent's site as part of her series, "Stealing Back Sabbath," September 18, 2014, https://tinyurl.com/y65f6ezo.

35 *Disciplines can "bring freedom":* Richard Foster, *Celebration of Discipline: The Path to Spiritual Growth* (New York: HarperOne, 1998), 2.

37 *Once the most Sabbatarian:* Judith Shulevitz, *The Sabbath World: Glimpses of a Different Order of Time* (New York: Random House, 2011), xxix.

38 *Massachusetts colony enacted:* Shulevitz, 147.

38 *Crackle with high drama:* Shulevitz, 145.

39 *The climax of our discoveries:* Maria Von Trapp, "The Land without a Sunday," *Fisheaters*, accessed May 10, 2020, https://

tinyurl.com/yy6brjgo. Originally appeared in *Around the Year with the Trapp Family* (New York: Pantheon, 1955).

41 *For the majority of clergy:* Trent, *For Sabbath's Sake*, 102.

CHAPTER 5

45 *Before I started:* I first explored some of the ideas in this chapter in a blog post I wrote entitled, "A Sabbath Retreat . . . But Where?" on author J. Dana Trent's site, August 25, 2017, https://tinyurl.com/yxco3kch.

48 *Scoop of moralizing smugness:* Ruth Whippman, "Actually, Let's Not Be in the Moment," *New York Times*, November 26, 2016, https://tinyurl.com/lqjgn5y.

49 *Defense against the pressures:* Whippman.

50 *Not so much about mastering silence:* Carl McColman, *The Big Book of Christian Mysticism: The Essential Guide to Contemplative Spirituality* (San Francisco: Hampton Roads, 2010), 218, 222.

50 *Constantly being swept off:* Foster, *Celebration of Discipline*, 27.

50 *Refers to a sense of balance:* Foster, 27.

51 *Too many anxious Christians:* Caryll Houselander, *A Child in Winter: Advent, Christmas, and Epiphany with Caryll Houselander*, ed. Thomas Hoffman (Franklin, WI: Sheed & Ward, 2000), 90.

CHAPTER 6

53 *Shift workers, including retail:* Kristin F. Butcher and Diane Whitmore Schanzenbach, "Most Workers in Low-Wage Labor Market Work Substantial Hours, in Volatile Jobs," Policy Futures, July 24, 2018, https://tinyurl.com/y4jopre7.

54 *When I was a parish minister:* Barbara Brown Taylor, "Letting God Run Things without My Help," *Christian Century*, May 5, 1999, https://tinyurl.com/y3awz8dk.

54 *The great day of equality:* Walter Brueggemann, *Sabbath as Resistance: Saying No to the Culture of Now* (Louisville: Westminster John Knox, 2017), 39–42.

54 *Research shows that Black Americans:* Brian Resnick, "The Racial Inequality of Sleep," *Atlantic*, October 27, 2015, https://tinyurl.com/ydcjvr9z.

54 *The "racial sleep gap":* William S. McFeely, *Frederick Douglass* (New York: W. W. Norton, 1995), 17.

55 *Body as a tool for production:* Maya Kroth, "It's a Right, Not a Privilege: The Napping Resistance Movement," Elemental, August 19, 2019, https://tinyurl.com/y6cge2wj.

55 *Harness and mimic the enormous:* J. Dana Trent, "Sabbath as Resistance," *Sojourners*, June 2018, https://tinyurl.com/yxvjducv.

55 *Troubling "merry-go-round":* Trent, *For Sabbath's Sake*, 106.

56 *Something is wrong, very wrong:* Barbara Ehrenreich, *Nickel and Dimed: On (Not) Getting By in America* (New York: Macmillan, 2002), 199.

People's level of happiness: Richard A. Easterlin et al., "The Happiness–Income Paradox Revisited," *Proceedings of the National Academy of Sciences* 107, no. 52 (December 28, 2010), https://tinyurl.com/y4ab6tln.

58 *An inward reality:* Foster, *Celebration of Discipline*, 79.

59 *Focus upon [God's] kingdom:* Foster, 87.

60 *Jesus declared war:* Foster, 82.

60 *Cancellation of $100 billion:* Charlotte Denny and Larry Elliot, "Debt Relief: Special Report Jubilee 2000—the Spark That Lit Global Revolt against Poverty," Global Policy Forum, December 1999, https://tinyurl.com/y6se6qgo.

60 *Supported by a diverse coalition:* Joshua Busby, "Is There a Constituency for Global Poverty? Jubilee 2000 and the Future of Development Advocacy," Brookings Institute, August 2002, https://tinyurl.com/y352bck3.

61 *The churches' finest hour:* Justin Welby, *Dethroning Mammon: Making Money Serve Grace* (London: Bloomsbury, 2016), 154.

61 *Poor countries are still struggling:* Mary Williams Walsh and Matt Phillips, "Poor Countries Face a Debt Crisis 'unlike Anything We Have Seen,'" *New York Times*, June 1, 2020, https://tinyurl.com/y4za4ynk.

CHAPTER 7

63 *Feelings of energy depletion:* "Burn-Out an Occupational Phenomenon: International Classification of Diseases," World Health Organization, May 28, 2019, https://tinyurl.com/y3mr2gq9.

64 *Dramatically increase our risk:* Jefferson Bethke, *To Hell with the Hustle: Reclaiming Your Life in an Overworked, Overspent, and Overconnected World* (Nashville: Thomas Nelson, 2019), 54.

64 *A myriad of illnesses:* Denise Albieri Jodas Salvagioni et al., "Physical, Psychological and Occupational Consequences of Job Burnout: A Systematic Review of Prospective Studies," *PLoS One* 12, no. 10 (October 4, 2017), https://tinyurl.com/y5nqcs28.

66 *Predictions indicate that by 2050:* Yemisi Adegoke, "UN: Half of World's Population Growth Is Likely to Occur in Africa," *CNN*, June 26, 2017, https://tinyurl.com/yywllvuw.

66 *Its Human Capital Index:* "Nigeria: Overview," World Bank, October 13, 2019, https://tinyurl.com/rgdkdj2.

66 *Second-largest HIV epidemic:* UNICEF, "UNICEF Nigeria Fact Sheets: An Overview of Key Thematic Areas," UNICEF Nigeria, July 2019, https://tinyurl.com/y6h6w7oc.

66 *3.3 million people displaced:* "Nigeria Emergency," UN Refugee Agency, 2020, https://tinyurl.com/w73h577.

67 *Fatima was sitting:* Bukola Adebayo, "Caught between Road-blocks, They Were Sitting Ducks for Boko Haram Massacre," *CNN*, February 15, 2020, https://tinyurl.com/y4b8ylrw.

68 *It is not a strange coincidence:* Ngũgĩ wa Thiong'o, "Learning from Slavery: The Legacy of the Slave Trade on Modern Society," UN Chronicle, January 2009, https://tinyurl.com/y4rvz7xy.

68 *From one century to the next:* Mary Elliott and Jazmine Hughes, "The 1619 Project," *New York Times*, August 19, 2019, https://tinyurl.com/y3jmbeo8.

69 *Commercial operations in Nigeria:* Esso Exploration & Production Nigeria Limited, *Exxon Mobile in Nigeria*, accessed February 20, 2020, https://tinyurl.com/y3w4rnlq.

70 *They had been slaves:* Rev. Dr. Howard-John Wesley, "December 1, 2019 'Selah,' Rev. Dr. Howard-John Wesley," Sermon at Alfred Street Baptist Church, YouTube video, December 4, 2019, https://tinyurl.com/y4qmpswv.

70 *Disrupts and pushes back:* Tricia Hersey, "Atlanta-Based Organization Advocates for Rest as a Form of Social Justice," interview by Sarah McCammon, NPR, June 4, 2020, https://tinyurl.com/y4fatbx3.

70 *White supremacy and capitalism:* Tricia Hersey, James Hamblin, and Katherine Wells, "Listen: You Are Worthy of Sleep. Even in a Pandemic," *Social Distance* podcast, April 30, 2020, https://tinyurl.com/y2ocwnkn.

CHAPTER 8

74 *Pray for us:* Houselander, *Child in Winter*, 73.
77 *A formal statement affirming:* "LGBTQ in the Church," Episcopal Church, 2020, https://episcopalchurch.org/lgbtq/history.
78 *If a pastor or youth pastor:* Amy Peterson, *Where Goodness Still Grows: Reclaiming Virtue in an Age of Hypocrisy* (Nashville: Thomas Nelson, 2020), 70–74.
79 *Course called About Your Sexuality:* The curriculum has been renamed "Our Whole Lives: Lifespan Sexuality Education," Unitarian Universalist Association, accessed July 1, 2020, https://www.uua.org/re/owl.
80 *The average adult:* Kate Julian, "The Sex Recession," *Atlantic*, December 2018, https://tinyurl.com/y97ec845.
83 *Greek schools of thought believed:* Bromleigh McCleneghan, *Good Christian Sex: Why Chastity Isn't the Only Option—and Other Things the Bible Says about Sex* (New York: HarperOne, 2016), 24–25.
83 *Fall into the same trap:* A. J. Swoboda, *Subversive Sabbath: The Surprising Power of Rest in a Nonstop World* (Grand Rapids, MI: Brazos, 2018), x.

CHAPTER 9

88 *Seeing a partial eclipse:* Annie Dillard, "Annie Dillard's Classic Essay: 'Total Eclipse,'" *Atlantic*, August 8, 2017, https://tinyurl.com/y7u9l9vk. Originally published 1982.
90 *Strong social skills and enjoy parties:* Susan Cain, *Quiet: The Power of Introverts in a World That Can't Stop Talking* (New York: Crown, 2013), 11, 136, 4–5.

91 *Universally recognized spiritual practices:* Elizabeth Gilbert, *Eat, Pray, Love: One Woman's Search for Everything across Italy, India and Indonesia* (New York: Penguin, 2006), 190.

92 *Dear God, I cannot love:* Flannery O'Connor, *A Prayer Journal* (New York: Farrar, Straus & Giroux, 2013), 3.

CHAPTER 10

98 *Not an escape from:* Swoboda, *Subversive Sabbath*, 58.

99 *Painful and destructive outcomes:* Swoboda, 59.

101 *The feeling of guilt:* Teia Collier, "Mom Guilt Is Real: Here's How to Beat It," ActiveKids, 2020, https://tinyurl.com/y3yo9g6d.

101 *As I paged through:* Lauren Smith Brody, "Why Mom Guilt Is the Biggest Lie of All," *Today's Parent*, April 5, 2020, https://tinyurl.com/yymd8xo4.

104 *How Coronavirus Exposes:* Jessica Grose, "How Coronavirus Exposes the Great Lie of Modern Motherhood," *New York Times*, March 25, 2020, https://tinyurl.com/y2p6sx38.

104 *Unwillingness to feel guilty:* For example, see Jennie Weiner, "I Refuse to Run a Coronavirus Home School," *New York Times*, March 19, 2020, https://tinyurl.com/yxymsvpz.

CHAPTER 11

108 *Fifty thousand times per month:* Alyssa Oursler, "The Work-Life Balance Fallacy," *Forbes*, July 27, 2015, https://tinyurl.com/y23lvoqt.

108 *I have always found:* Maria Popova, "Poet and Philosopher David Whyte on Fulfillment beyond the Limiting Notion of Work/Life Balance," Brainpickings, March 2015, https://tinyurl.com/y5rea4ko.

109 *Impoverish them all:* David Whyte, *The Three Marriages: Reimagining Work, Self and Relationship* (New York: Penguin, 2009), iv.

110 *A fascinating harmony:* Swoboda, *Subversive Sabbath*, 56.

110 *Parenting is not confined:* Claire Cain Miller, "Three Things Lockdowns Have Exposed about Working and Parenting," *New York Times*, April 27, 2020, https://tinyurl.com/y2h4nca4.

111 *Recognize the need:* Miller.

112 *Debate over the minimum wage:* Benjamin J. Dueholm, "The War against Rest," *Christian Century*, November 17, 2014, https://tinyurl.com/yxkss9sn.

112 *After Fernandes's death:* Rachel L. Swarns, "For a Worker with Little Time between 3 Jobs, a Nap Has Fatal Consequences," *New York Times*, September 28, 2014, https://tinyurl.com/y6zk9ezj.

112 *Idea that the price of labor:* Dueholm, "War against Rest."

112 *Modern day animal agriculture:* Lewis Regenstein, *The Bible's Teachings on Protecting Animals and Nature*, Humane Society of the United States, 2006, https://tinyurl.com/v2h78mn.

CHAPTER 12

117 *World Health Organization recognized:* "Coronavirus Disease (COVID-19) Pandemic," World Health Organization, 2020, https://tinyurl.com/yyc68g6n.

118 *Even if we knew the exact date:* Sleeth, 24/6, 22–23.

120 *Let the servants of the Lord:* Wilson B. Bishai, "Sabbath Observance from Coptic Sources," *Andrews University Seminary Studies* 1, no. 1 (1963): 25–31, https://tinyurl.com/yys57mgp.

123 *Help us live "resurrection lives":* Ruth Valerio, *Saying Yes to Life* (London: SPCK, 2019), 169.

123 *Activity of being a church:* Norman Wirzba, *Living the Sabbath: Discovering the Rhythms of Rest and Delight* (Grand Rapids, MI: Brazos, 2006), 49.

CHAPTER 13

125 *The phrase* time confetti*:* Brigid Schulte, *Overwhelmed: How to Work, Love, and Play When No One Has the Time* (New York: Picador, 2014), 9.

126 *Not just "indulgent 'yuppie kvetch'":* Schulte, 9.

126 *Overwhelmed, in poorer health:* Schulte, 27, 19.

127 *Strong enough to compel:* Wesley Morris, "The Videos That Rocked America. The Song That Knows Our Rage," *New York Times*, June 3, 2020, https://tinyurl.com/y49rh5ax.

128 *Prayer and action must:* Kerri Lenartowick, "Always Unite Prayer and Action, Pope Francis Says," *Catholic News Agency*, July 21, 2013, https://tinyurl.com/yyqoc7t5.

129 *Includes seven key components:* There are many great sources that describe this simple, classic prayer structure. The exact components and the order vary depending on the source you read. For example, see W. G. Scroggie, *Quiet Time: A Practical Guide for Daily Devotions* (Carol Stream, IL: InterVarsity, 1947).

131 *We confess that we have sinned:* "A Penitential Order: Rite One," *Book of Common Prayer*, accessed June 15, 2020, https://www.bcponline.org/HE/penord1.html.

133 *Problem to be solved rather:* Schulte, *Overwhelmed*, 277–78.

CHAPTER 14

135 *Estimated 120 emails per day:* André Spicer, "How Many Work Emails Is Too Many?," *Guardian*, April 8, 2019, https://tinyurl .com/y67ku3tz.

136 *Refers to as "deep work":* Cal Newport, *Deep Work: Rules for Focused Success in a Distracted World* (New York: Grand Central, 2016).

137 *In an open marketplace for attention:* Cal Newport, *Digital Minimalism: Choosing a Focused Life in a Noisy World* (New York: Penguin, 2019), xii.

137 *Jesus was so often interrupted:* "Ministry Interruptions," World Renew, November 2, 2017, https://tinyurl.com/y54la3ef.

138 *Companies are starting to experiment:* Kelsey Gee, "Sunday Night Is the New Monday Morning, and Workers Are Miserable," *Wall Street Journal,* July 7, 2019, https://tinyurl.com/yya7ybsv.

138 *Calls for digital Sabbaths:* For example, see the Digital Sabbath Project, A Faithtech Labs project, accessed August 15, 2020, https://digitalsabbath.io/.

138 *Reduces available cognitive capacity:* Tim Herrera, "Hide Your Phone When You're Trying to Work. Seriously," *New York Times*, December 2, 2018, https://tinyurl.com/ycbo6yfm.

139 *How slick and weasel-like:* Thomas Kelley, *A Testament of Devotion* (1941; repr., San Francisco: HarperOne, 1996), 62.

139 *Bring our sincere prayers:* Inge Schmidt, "Praying the News," *Christian Science Monitor*, October 29, 2019, https://tinyurl .com/y4a4xr8j.

140 *It is one thing to race:* Abraham J. Herschel, *The Sabbath* (1951; repr., New York: HarperOne, 1997), 29.

141 *Americans who practice yoga:* Alice G. Walton, "How Yoga Is Spreading in the U.S.," *Forbes*, March 15, 2016, https://tinyurl .com/y3j2xr9c.

142 *The coming kingdom of God:* Verna J. Dozier, *The Dream of God: A Call to Return* (New York: Seabury, 2006), 85, 5.

CHAPTER 15

147 *Run for leisure:* Morris, "Videos That Rocked."

149 *Progressive philosophy of life:* "Definition of Humanism," American Humanist Society, accessed June 30, 2020, https://tinyurl.com/ybwhrhvo.

150 *Building of a more humane society:* "Definition of Humanism."

150 *The field of mental health:* David Rademacher, "Buddhism and Psychotherapy," accessed June 30, 2020, https://davidrademacher.com/?p=49.

152 *Two popular versions:* N. T. Wright, *After You Believe: Why Christian Character Matters* (New York: HarperOne, 2010), 66.

152 *Idea of a disembodied heaven:* Wright, 66.

152 *Establish God's kingdom:* Wright, 66–67.

154 *Kingdom and cross belong together:* Wright, 116–17.

154 *Lynching tree joined the cross:* James H. Cone, *The Cross and the Lynching Tree* (Maryknoll, NY: Orbis, 2011), 3.

155 *Under extreme pressure:* Cone, 84.

155 *Nonviolence was more:* Cone, 85.

155 *Paradox of the crucified savior:* Cone, 1.

156 *Taught that humans:* Wright, *After You Believe*, 116.

156 *Virtue we view "as self-made":* Wright, 116.

160 *I remain vulnerable to despair:* Kathleen Norris, *Amazing Grace: A Vocabulary of Faith* (New York: Penguin, 1998), 181.

CHAPTER 16

\\\\\\\\\\\\\\\\\\\\\\\\\\\\\\\\\\

164 *By junior year:* My mother, Lynn Holbein, was interviewed and
quoted in this book by Thelma Reese and B. J. Kittredge, *How
Seniors Are Saving the World: Retirement Activism to the Rescue*
(Lanham, MD: Rowman & Littlefield, 2020), 62.

166 *Fundamental conflict of interest:* David L. Chappell, *A Stone of
Hope: Prophetic Religion and the Death of Jim Crow* (Chapel
Hill: University of North Carolina Press, 2004), 31.

167 *I think that I have a higher power:* Reese and Kittredge, *How
Seniors Are Saving the World,* 66.

167 *I live by the serenity prayer:* Reese and Kittredge, 68.

169 *Power of human reason:* Chappell, *Stone of Hope,* 3, 86.

169 *Moral improvements of the world:* Chappell, 3.

169 *Driven not by modern liberal faith:* Chappell, 3.

169 *The prophetic ideas:* Chappell, 44, 86.

170 *Did not win all of their goals:* Chappell, 8.

170 *Liberal and prophetic ideas complicates:* Chappell, 83.

CHAPTER 17

\\\\\\\\\\\\\\\\\\\\\\\\\\\\\\\\\\

181 *Astounded by the fact:* Wirzba, *Living the Sabbath,* 37.

174 *A British Parliamentarian:* Christopher Leslie Brown, *Moral
Capital: Foundations of British Abolitionism* (Chapel Hill: University of North Carolina Press, 2006).

174 *An ardent Sabbatarian:* Brown.

175 *Suffered from health problems:* Gordon MacDonald, *Ordering
Your Private World* (Nashville: Thomas Nelson, 2007), 191.

176 *Lauren Winner explains:* Lauren H. Winner, *The Dangers of
Christian Practice* (New Haven: Yale University Press, 2018).

177 *One woman's justice:* Mychal Denzel Smith, "The Truth about 'The Arc of the Moral Universe,'" *Huffington Post*, January 18, 2018, https://tinyurl.com/yx9h6yjk.

177 *The sinfulness of the world:* Winner, *Dangers of Christian Practice*, 158.

180 *Veil's primary function:* D. M. Gurtner, "The Veil Was Torn: What Really Happened on Good Friday?," Desiring God, April 19, 2019, https://tinyurl.com/y2mkaxg2.

181 *Oh God . . . grant that:* Episcopal Church, *The Book of Common Prayer and Administration of the Sacraments and Other Rites and Ceremonies of the Church* (New York: Seabury, 1979), 282.

181 *Triumph of all humanity:* John Dominic Crossan and Sarah Crossan, *Resurrecting Easter: How the West Lost and the East Kept the Original Easter Vision* (New York: HarperCollins, 2018), 72.

QUICK-START GUIDE TO SABBATH KEEPING

185 *A universe without God:* Robert South Barrett, *A Reason of the Hope* (Washington, DC: National Publishing Company, 1896), 98.

187 *Our family has summed it:* Swoboda, *Subversive Sabbath*, 39.

187 *Consider engaging in activities:* Swoboda, 57.

188 *Devices in the same room:* Herrera, "Hide Your Phone."

188 *Move beyond tweaks:* Newport, *Digital Minimalism*, 27–28.

190 *Composed of twenty-one distinct units:* Donna Schaper, *Keeping Sabbath*, pamphlet, Forward Movement, 2018.

191 *Dawn has some good suggestions:* Marva J. Dawn, *Keeping the Sabbath Wholly* (Grand Rapids, MI: Eerdmans, 1989).

191 *O God of peace:* Episcopal Church, *Book of Common Prayer*, 282.

191 *God did not give this commandment:* Barbara Brown Taylor, "Sabbath Resistance: Sabbath and the Status Quo," *Christian Century*, May 31, 2005, https://tinyurl.com/y2tkh3hg.

192 *Like a 500-piece jigsaw puzzle:* MaryAnn McKibben Dana, *Sabbath in the Suburbs: A Family's Experiment with Holy Time* (St. Louis, MO: Chalice, 2012), 2.